Mercy Rewrote My Life

Sadie Brunson

The Best is yet to Come
for you
The Lord

DMJ Publishing & Web Design, Delaware

Sadie Brunson

First edition copyright ©2008 Sadie Brunson

ISBN 10: 0-615-23152-7
ISBN 13: 978-0-615-23152-5

Published by DMJ Publishing & Web Design, Delaware
In cooperation with SelfPublishing.com

Cover Design by:
Tynetta Clemment
Email: tbratten01@comcast.net
Tel: (302) 293-6006

Printed in the United States of America

Unless otherwise identified, all scriptural references are taken from the New International Version (NIV) and the King James Version (KJV) of the Bible.

This book is lovingly dedicated to God for allowing me to see my enemies, love them and deal with them correctly.

As you read this book, be careful to absorb every word because God has sent His anointing to set you free. God has prepared a victory for you over your hurt and over your pain.

I love you and I pray that this book will be the key to the release of your pain. I pray you hear my heart.

Father, help me to understand that the punishment and repercussions that come to people when they have done wrong is often sufficient for them. Instead of causing more grief, your Word says I ought to forgive and comfort the person so that he or she will not be overwhelmed by excessive sorrow. (2 Cor. 2:7) Lord, help me to be the kind of person I want ministering to me after I have failed.

-- Sadie Brunson --

Acknowledgments

My special thanks to my mother, Mary Morgan; daughters Tracy, Nichole, Marlene; son Michael; and brother Ira Shy who have labored faithfully.

My love and gratitude to all those God has used to support, encourage and impart into my life including but not limited to Pastors Gary and Faye Whetstone, Beverly "Bam" Crawford, Bishop T.D. Jakes (Woman Thou Art Loosed), Myles Munroe, Savanna Collins, Fay Dadzie, Gladys Dixon, Kathy Turner, Donna Maxwell, Cornell Brunson, Larry De Jarnette, Wilbert Moultrie, Alan Brown, Jabbar Shy, Jabbar Jr., Helen Lowery, Women Aglow, Abundant Love Ministries, Sadie's & Co., Nichole Tatuem, Dr. Caren Thompson, Mary Cooper, B. T. Thomas, Marsha Benton, Pastor Jeanette Ford, Gary and Joy Hill, Forrest and Denise Watson, Robert Pointer, Robert Eubanks, Alkay Williams, Saundra Hagans, Keith Tucker and Renee Richerson.

I acknowledge with joy the growing wisdom in the body of Christ. My special thanks to Apostle Thomas Wesley Weeks, Sr. and my family, New Destiny Fellowship.

My special thanks to Donna Jacobs who had patience and encouragement as we struggled to complete the writing and transcription prior to publishing this book. I also acknowledge and thank First Lady Tamara T. Scott, Freda Wilson and Pastor Iris Perkins who lovingly assisted with editing this book.

FOREWORD

Pastor Sadie Brunson has led a remarkable life. She has been to the gates of hell and back. She has been left for dead; the devil thought he would never hear from her again. Did he get the surprise of his life! She is alive and doing well and telling her story.

Her story is the story of us; how satan lied to us and had us believing things that were destroying us. At our worst moment, we heard a call from the Savior and received Him as the Lord of our lives. With the call of Jesus on our lives, we began a journey to receive our deliverance and to walk in the full freedom and joy of God.

However, our story is still under attack from the devil and the journey is not over. He is still lying and deceiving and doing his best to sabotage the Will of God for our lives. For us to overcome this assault by the enemy, we must be able to walk in truth. Truth will set us free. However, someone must be courageous enough to bare his or her life as an open book so others can learn the truth about the devil's lies. This book is the answer to that need.

Pastor Brunson's life story will have us crying, rejoicing, believing, but most importantly, knowing what God did for her, He will do for us. Be prepared to walk away from the lies and failures of the past and into a victorious future. Thank you for telling us the truth, Pastor Brunson.

Thomas Wesley Weeks, Sr.

Sadie Brunson

Table of Contents

Sadie Brunson

Chapter 1

In the Beginning

The warm safety of my surroundings made me a trusting child who loved and enjoyed life without fear in the bosom of my family and friends. Until one day a trusted family friend, a pastor, touched me in a way that no friend or no shepherd should.

He came to steal my innocence; to feed his own lust for pleasure and power. In a moment's time he shattered my peace of mind, took my glow and left me confused. I didn't know what to do or how to tell anyone what happened. I was molested. And everyday I had to go to this person's house.

The little girl had been abused and violated by the one whom they all knew as Pastor, someone everybody loved and trusted. Although I was only a child and had done nothing wrong, I felt guilty and ashamed.

I wanted to tell my mother but he was my mother's friend, someone she loved and trusted, so I just put my wounds inside thinking they would go away. But they never went away.

As a child I was stripped of self-esteem, joy, trust and the belief that I was beautiful. It was hard for me to trust anyone again, including the Lord. I felt unworthy, dirty, lonely, guilty and ashamed.

One ungodly touch changed my destiny and I walked with a spiritual limp. That's why I can relate to the story of Jonathan's son, Mephibosheth, a prince of Israel who was lame in his feet. Mephibosheth was wounded as a child while in the hands of a trusted servant. He was five years old just as I was. You can read the story about this young man who had a limp in 2 Samuel, Chapter 4.

I have been counseled and prayed for extensively. I got so weary of hiding this issue of woundedness that I searched out the destiny God had on the inside of me in spite of the pain. I always knew there was something great in me.

There are so many boys and girls who have been wounded in one way or another. They gather together for fellowship, as if attending a masquerade ball, hiding behind religious masks of wholeness. Behind the masks, resides great pain that has caused them to be spiritually limp.

Living with hidden issues leads us to spend our whole lives proving we're someone else to the Church, living with a spiritual limp. Sometimes we end up in relationships that lead to even more abuse. None of this is God's design. God did not choose for us to walk through life spiritually lame or wounded by our past.

God does not desire for us to live in separation and limitations. Somehow the abused ones convince themselves that this is God's plan for their lives. That is truly a lie. This reminds me of the thief we find in God's word in John 10:10 who comes to steal, kill and destroy the great destiny God has for us. We think we must learn to live with the pain. But I found out in the scriptures that Jesus came to give us abundant life. What purpose, what glory could there be for a person to live under the power or the influence of wounds?

God calls himself JEHOVAH ROPHE, the Lord our Healer; we find that in Exodus 15:26, "...for I am the Lord that healeth thee." He is the one who puts us back together when we are wounded.

I want to tell you a few things about the little girl I was talking about who was left with a trusted friend. That little girl was me. And that little girl was trapped in a body with so many issues and so many wounds caused by past hurts. She was afraid to come out. What would people think of her? Even at that age, the enemy knew how to stop her. The enemy often comes when we're young because we have no defenses. We don't know who we are. He comes to abort our destiny because he knows there's something great in us.

So I went on a journey. On this journey, I was hiding from myself. I looked for deliverance. I looked for love in all the wrong places. I remember going to psychiatrists and trying to find out what my problem was. At a very early age, the pain manifested because I felt so unloved. I felt so rejected. It began to manifest in stealing.

Sadie Brunson

Chapter 2

My Addiction

I want to share a little bit about what happens to a child when the enemy comes in. When the enemy comes in, he leaves scars and wounds. He leaves rejection and abandonment. A lot of things began to happen to me. I began to steal at a very early age. The first thing I stole was a peach. One of the little boys in the neighborhood taught me how to steal. When I stole the peach, I gave it to a friend. That friend just received me and hugged me and thanked me.

I thought I did a great thing because somebody seemed to approve of me and like me. So I began to steal even bigger things. Thus the journey of stealing began. At first, it was fun. Then it became uncontrollable.

I would steal almost every day. It was like a high. It was very exciting. I was in my own little world. I began to steal small things and then bigger and bigger things until one day I ended up in girls' school. That was a great thing because when I ended up in girls' school, I met new friends. The friends I met were all problem children that had been dropped by society.

I was a very young girl but I began to communicate with them. I found out that five of them had been molested. Of course, I didn't tell them I was also molested. I couldn't say such a thing because the one who molested me was so honorable. He was a pastor. How could I say that? They would think I was crazy. Everybody looked up to pastors. There was such shame on me, like I was the one who had done something wrong. I knew that while I was in girls' school, I was in a safe place. It was a safe place because I didn't have to be around that person.

Sadie Brunson

I ended up learning a lot about life through these young girls. I learned about their pain and how they hated to go home. All of us had the same issue but we were different. They wanted to know why I kept coming back to girls' school when I had a good home to go to.

I did come from a very good home. I only had one brother. We were probably poor but we didn't know it because we had everything. I had a mother who worked very hard to make sure we had everything. She was a very loving and kind woman. I always thought my mother was the prettiest woman in the world. She took very good care of me and my brother.

There are a lot of good things I can say about my childhood because my mother taught me the word of God. She taught me about God when I was very little but I was still confused. I always wondered why God would let something like this happen to me. I had to live in this shell and I couldn't tell my mother. I couldn't tell my brother whom I loved. All I did was steal. They seemed to be happy I stole because I would bring things home and no one would ever make me take them back. I felt like it was okay to steal. I don't know if my mother knew I stole or not but I always had things.

What I remember most of all was the woman who ran the girls' school. She once said to me, "There's something wrong in your home because you're a very nice girl. You shouldn't be here." She would always give me compliments. She used to tell me I was smart. She would ask me, "Why don't you like school?" I told her I couldn't concentrate in school.

It was like there was a spirit or a cloud over me. Part of me was one way and part of me was another way. It was like the enemy robbed me. He was always in my mind; he was always telling me where to steal and how to steal. A force that I couldn't see was controlling me. Later in life, I found out it was demon. I didn't know how to rid myself of this entity that grew so big inside of me. It constantly controlled my life.

The woman who ran the girls' school sent me to a psychiatrist because everyone wanted to know what my problem was. The courts wanted to know why I stole. Because I had everything, they knew I didn't have to steal. But it was like a never-ending battle. I would go through the motions. I would go back and forth to psychiatrists for counseling. This continued for a period of about 10 years. When I left girls' school, I graduated to prison.

I was also sent to the state hospital for about two months. They placed me in the state hospital to find out what was wrong with me. I was never given medication but I was there among all kinds of people who had all kinds of problems. It was very spooky. I had to see doctors everyday. I had to talk to them but I never really told them the truth because I could never say that this man, who everyone respected, was the person who molested me. I didn't realize then what goes into a person when they get molested but it's a serious thing.

While I was at the state hospital, I saw so many wounded people. I was always a caring and loving person behind the masks I wore. It was as if I were two people. Part of me was loving and the other part of me was a thief. At that time, I don't think it bothered me too much. When I began to see those people in the state hospital, I knew one day I was going to come back to help them. That was the kind of heart I had, even as a thief.

Because I felt so unloved, I wanted people to like me. I was such a hypocrite since I lived two lives. I felt like I was the only person in the world who had this issue because I kept it a secret for so long.

When you keep a secret for a long time, you feel like you're the only one in the world like you. I never looked outward to see that other people had the same problem; not even when I went to prison and to the state hospital. I saw all these people with problems but I still thought I was the only one with this problem. In prison, they blamed and hated everybody. It was a horrible atmosphere but I could see that we all had the same pain. I fit in so nicely because I was with people who couldn't help themselves. Nobody really cared about them; they just put them away. They were very angry and bitter.

Even though I had my issues, I never grew angry or bitter. I just thought something was so wrong with me that I would live like this for the rest of my life. At court, one of the judges told me I was a kleptomaniac and I thought maybe I was. I was sick. I couldn't talk to my friends about it because they didn't know about my secret lifestyle. One day I would be with them and then I'd disappear by the next day because of the double life I led. I would go to prison and meet new friends there. It was a lifestyle for me.

Even writing this story, I never knew how I really felt until right now. I never went over this story enough to know that it was a way of life for me. Finally, I fit in. When I went home, I would always be glad to be with my mother and brother. But I always had to steal, feeling that they would like me if I gave them something. I wanted to be loved and accepted but I didn't know why I wanted to be accepted. I really wanted to change, but I thought that was impossible.

I became very good at being a thief. It became like a profession because I felt like there was nothing I couldn't steal. I had all kinds of money. I remember when I was about 12 years old, I stole a large sum of money. In my mind, I really didn't steal it. I found it. I took it home to my brother and it was more money than I could count.

I remember taking a one hundred dollar bill downtown to give to this white, homeless lady who always stood in front of the Dry Goods store. People would laugh at her. I wanted to be her friend but she didn't want me as her friend. I dropped the hundred dollar bill and said "Lady, you dropped that". She picked it up and said "Oh my". She grabbed my hand and said, "Thank you." She actually hugged me. It was like wow! I finally won her over; she really liked me. I would have given anything to make somebody like me. At the time, I didn't realize there was a spirit within me constantly telling me nobody loved me or cared about me.

Every now and then I would get very sad about my lifestyle. When I had to go to the psychiatrists, they would bring it up so I was aware of my behavior. I was aware of being a thief, but now pride had kicked in because I could get whatever I wanted. Today, it would be equivalent to the mindset of a drug dealer. Once you begin making money, it becomes an addiction and you just can't stop. I became smarter; I was in my own little world.

Sadie Brunson

Chapter 3

First Encounter

When I was in my teens, I played with doll babies and paper dolls. I lived in my head and always lied to myself. Those paper dolls and doll babies were my best friends. I had about a hundred doll babies and I would constantly amuse myself with them. I couldn't imagine going to a dance or being normal like other girls. But when I was 15, I was invited to go to a school dance at Salesianum. It was very different for me; it was nothing like the dances that I went to at the Hotel du Pont. An awesome young man asked me to dance. He really showed me how to have a good time. I believe I was the prettiest young lady at the party.

He told me he loved me. That was the most awesome thing anybody could have ever said to me. Because remember, I was the one who was looking for love in all the wrong places. I didn't know anything about being with a man, absolutely nothing. The only thing I knew about a man was that one molested me and I really didn't remember much about that because I had blocked it out of my mind.

This guy told me he loved me and the next thing I knew we were in the backseat of his car. I was so silly. I went home and told my mother what happened because I didn't know any better. Six months had gone by before I found out I was pregnant. I had never experienced anything like that in my life. My girlfriends, Vy and Teenie, who I'd met at the party were the ones who told me I was pregnant.

I led a crazy life because I didn't know much about living since I grew up sheltered and kept to myself. I did know a few things about sex that I learned from my friends at girls' school. At the time, I thought I was better than they were because they sold themselves. They were like prostitutes. They did anything to survive and anything to stay away from home. Really, I wasn't any better than they were because I stole and didn't even care if I got caught. There were times I thought it would make me happier if someone did catch me because I was tired of stealing.

Somehow, I always felt convicted about stealing; it felt so wrong. During all my escapades, I still continued to go to church. I found out that you reap what you sow. Every Sunday I would go to the altar and ask God to forgive me. I always thought I had to pay for my sins. I didn't know that God would forgive me. I had no idea that Jesus had already paid for my sins a long time ago (Romans 6:23). I had no clue. At that time, I didn't know anything about the power of deliverance. I would find myself begging God to forgive me as I would cry, and cry, and cry. There was a spirit living inside of me that was good and there was a spirit living inside of me that was bad. I felt like I could never win because they continually warred against each other (Galatians 5:17). When I got caught stealing and sent back to girls' school or to prison, I thought I was paying for my sins and it made me feel better. I didn't know anything about the power of forgiveness. I knew what I was doing was wrong but I didn't know how to change.

When I went to prison, I was hiding. It really wasn't a bad prison. It was more like a little house with mothers who took care of me. That's where I learned how to cook, sew, draw and set up tables. Interestingly enough, I learned many marvelous things in prison which included how to interact with people. When people made mistakes, I was able to show them love and still speak kindly to them. I was a big talker in prison but I was shy on the street. I felt like everybody knew me so I couldn't be myself. I was very shy and stayed to myself for a very long time.

My self-esteem was very low because I never really went to school. When I was taken out of school periodically, I was ashamed because I was always behind. Since I wasn't a high achiever in school and could never remember what I'd learned, I didn't like it. There were certain things I couldn't remember because I wanted to block them out. When I was in prison, I went to school but it was very different. I could take any of the classes I wanted to take. My academic skills were not good, but I was very skilled with my hands. Since I could sew and cook well, those were the classes I took.

The lifestyle I kept living grew progressively worse. Around 1971, my minor misdemeanors became felonies. By this time I had my first child, Tracy. When I gave birth to her, I didn't feel emotional at all. I'd gotten pregnant this time because I wanted to be loved. I was so devastated when her father denied her. He said she wasn't his child. What a rejection! When my mother and I took him to court for child support, he showed up with his family. He told the judge she wasn't his child. The judge ordered him to pay me $8 per week. I was so devastated about the entire situation that I left the courtroom. I thought it was the worst thing that could have ever happened to me. It was difficult to believe this person who told me he loved me would do this.

I didn't understand love even though it's something we're all created to give and receive. Just hearing the words made me feel better, until he rejected me. I left that courtroom feeling so wounded. From that moment on, my inner demon took over. I really began to steal. Not that I wasn't stealing already but now I wanted to prove I could take care of this child on my own. Stealing became my career. It's what I did for a living.

Except for that first time with James, I never stole with other people. I never went stealing with a girlfriend or a team, because I was ashamed of it. I would hop the train and go out of town to steal. There wasn't anything or anyone who could hold me back now because I knew how to get to different places without assistance. I was a well-traveled teenager.

Chapter 4

Marriage #1

I finally got married. As a young woman, I was blessed in spite of my way of life. I knew God had to be with me because He would always say, "Don't do that!" I used to say, "Shut up, who's that talking to me?" Whenever I proceeded to do wrong after hearing Him say, "Don't do that", I would get caught. I didn't know at that time it was God speaking to me because I was told that God didn't speak to sinners. So I used to tell that voice to shut up because I knew it couldn't be God. I didn't think He cared about people like me. I didn't know He died for me nor did I know He loved me in spite of the way I acted. I thought God would never allow a little girl to be molested. I thought He would never let a little girl live in such shame and guilt. I just didn't know, so I didn't believe.

During that time, I attended Victory Christian Fellowship. A prophet told me that God had called me. She told me I was going to be the one. That I was the one in my family who was chosen to do all these great things and to set the captives free. I thought she was crazy but I sat and listened to her. She told me I needed to stop trying to hide behind all these different things, like marriage. I knew she was right but I couldn't stop because I didn't know how to stop. I left Victory and stayed away for a whole year.

I went back to my old church. When I went back to my old church, they loved me. This time it was different. There was real love there. But when you've been rejected, you don't know how to receive love because you've never had it.

Sadie Brunson

My marriage didn't work because I married someone like me. He was addicted to drugs; I was addicted to stealing. It was difficult to understand that a person attracts what they are. I didn't understand why I kept getting nice people in my life but then found out we couldn't live together. We had two daughters together, Nikki and Marlene. Right after I had Nikki, I found out I was pregnant with Marlene. That was hard for me.

I went to prison while we were married. This time it was more serious because the judge gave me a year at the women's prison. While I was there, I met this awesome woman and we became friends. She was one of my best friends in prison. It wasn't such a bad thing to be in prison because I had fun. She was there for three years and I was there for a year. We crocheted together, ate dinner together and worked together. We were like two silly little kids. But I never dealt with my issues. I just went to prison and did my time. Since I didn't deal with my issues, they got bigger.

When I got out, I went home and ended up getting a divorce. My husband had gotten into a relationship with another woman and she was pregnant. We sold our house and I moved into an apartment. During all the times I went to prison, I never lost my children. I was always blessed to be able to keep my children together with family and friends, especially with the mothers of the church back then. They were very loving to me.

I was a young girl then but I was a thief so I saved a lot of money. I saved money because I always knew I was going to go to prison. The money I saved was for lawyers and to take care of my children.

Mercy Rewrote My Life

I had gone back to my old church because I missed my friends. But the Lord spoke to me and said, "If you don't get out of this church, your daughters will grow up sleeping around." I heard God. He spoke to me and I took my children out of that church. I heard God say, "Get out of there!" The man that molested me was dead but his spirit was still in that church. The deacons in that church slept around with anybody. It didn't bother them that their actions hurt people.

When I was in that church, the biggest lie was told on me while I was pregnant with my daughter, Marlene. I was a married woman but a man at the church told everyone I was pregnant by him. Unfortunately, a lot of the church people believed him. This devastated me because I never slept around. I believed in the sanctity of marriage. At that time in my life, I'd never done anything like that but I was accused of it. One day this woman looked me in the face and said, "I know you didn't do that because I know your character." That blessed me more than anything else, that somebody knew my character.

I was able to stand in front of a whole group of people at church and tell them I didn't do it. But that didn't matter. I felt better because I knew God was with me. After that, the man's wife came to me and said, "I know you didn't do that." I thank God that He revealed this to her. Sometime after that happened and I had returned to Victory Christian Fellowship, that same man came to me with his wife and asked if I could tell him how to receive the baptism of the Holy Spirit. Without hesitation, I led him through the steps to receive the baptism of the Holy Spirit. I will never forget that day. Even though I'd been lied on and struggled through a period of hurt, God still carried me through in order to minister His love to another.

My journey wasn't over yet. I was still an addicted person. I was still a thief. I still lied to myself. And I still didn't know how to deal with my children.

Chapter 5

Marriage #2

Things began to change after my divorce. At that time, my kids were in Christian schools and I was a barmaid. However, I still took my kids to church every Sunday. One day, after service, I was standing in the church parking lot. I said "God, if you really are God, I don't want to be a barmaid anymore. I can't sleep at night and my eyes hurt. What did you call me to do in this world?" I heard this voice say, "Go to beauty school." Immediately, I went home, changed and went to the Academy of Hair Design. They told me it would cost $500. Of course, in 1972 that was a lot of money. That year was an awesome year for me because I knew God had told me to go to beauty school. I was a sinner but yet, He spoke to me. That really amazed me.

I got married for the second time by the end of 1972. Right after the wedding, I got pregnant again with my son, Michael, who was born with meningitis. He had yellow jaundice and a large head and needed a lot of care. At 24 years old, I remember lying in the hospital room crying and asking God why He would give me this child when He knew I had so many issues already. I was crying so hard that they didn't tie my tubes because they thought maybe I wanted another child. Boy, was I hurt. At the time, I had a serious court case pending. There were three felonies against me. I was in a terrible predicament. I kept asking God why He would give me a child like this when I was all messed up?

Two girls from the church came to see me and caught me crying very hard. They wanted to know why I was crying. I told them I didn't know why God would give me a child like Michael when I had so many other issues. I knew I had to go to court and that I would probably have to go to jail again. One of the girls, Maryann, said to me, "Sadie, God gave you this child because you will love him." She told me I was the most loving person in the world. That was so nice of her to say. So many people told me I was loving and kind but I couldn't see any of that. The only thing I could see was my pain. I wanted to be loved but I was so miserable, so rejected, and so afraid. I had these three little girls at home that deserved a better mom and all I could give them was a life of lies. They didn't even know what kind of person their mother really was.

They were so special to me. They were the best little girls any mother could have. They were very obedient and sweet. Nikki was feisty. Tracy was different. She loved church. Nikki and Marlene loved church too. Nikki was the one I knew would always pray for me because she was the one who would speak up and speak out. She wrote the Lord a letter when she was 9 years old and asked Him to save her mother. I'll never forget that. God answered her prayers because when I went to jail in 1972, the judge sentenced me to three years, which turned out to be the most time I ever received. It was horrific!! I was then a homeowner who had furs, diamonds and Cadillacs. I had everything, yet my world was crumbling. I also had a little baby who needed me more than life. With that said, let me tell you about the mercy of God.

A church lady came to the prison on my first day there. She was a white woman. She asked the warden if she could take me to church and the warden said yes. So she took me to church. We went to this home called Sweetness House. It was a Jesus group, a charismatic group of women and men. The house was loaded with people. They were singing in the spirit and worshiping the Lord. I had never seen anything like that. They were worshiping with their hands lifted up, just loving Jesus.

When I walked into that atmosphere, it felt like I was home. I don't know what happened but they ended up leading me to the Lord. I had been led to the Lord many times but this time was different. This time I gave Him my heart. I went into a beautiful language, a heavenly language. I began to speak in tongues but I didn't know it was a tongue at the time. Everybody was doing it. They were interpreting and they began to prophesy over me. They began to speak life and that was the first time anyone had ever done that for me. I felt like I was being taken out of myself. It was like an out of body experience. It was like a presence that I didn't want to ever leave me. It was so awesome how God just came in. I know He did something for me that day.

I felt like it was because I obeyed Him when she asked, "Do you accept Him to be Lord over your life?" I can hear it today just like it was yesterday. I said, "yes". When I said yes, faith kicked in but I didn't understand it. The only thing I did was obey. When I went back to prison that night, I was so happy. I was singing the songs that they were singing. They sang these songs called "Jesus, Jesus" and "If It Weren't for the Lighthouse, Where Would I Be".

Such worship! I was from a black church and we didn't worship the Lord. I sang on the choir but we didn't worship the Lord. In 1972, I learned how to worship my Father. It was the most awesome experience. Those songs would just ring in me and I would lift my hands to the Lord. It seemed like His presence would just come. They taught me that when I raised my hands to the Lord, I lifted my heart to Him. I never forgot those things.

On the way back to prison, the lady from Sweetness House gave me my first Christian book. It was called "The Power of Praise". I read that book every day. I was a slow reader but I read that book in two days. I read it over and over again. I learned to give thanks in everything I go through. I found out that my destiny is in His hands. I didn't understand it but I read it in that book. I learned the spirit of thanksgiving, and how God forgave me for all my sins. They told me that when I fall He will pick me up. They taught me about the righteousness of Christ Jesus and that it wasn't me that was right; it was Him that was right. I didn't understand everything but I remembered those things that meant so much to me.

When I went back to prison that night, I went back happy. I was laughing and singing and my roommates Vicky and Joanie laughed at me. Vicky was so beautiful. She was a young beautiful woman in prison who had issues like me. Joanie was beautiful too. We were three beautiful women in our twenties. Joanie was a white girl who was very wealthy and had horses but she still had issues. We were in the room together and they were talking about jailhouse religion and saying it wasn't going to last.

I believe Vicky had five years, Joanie had about five years and I had three. When I prayed that night, the Holy Spirit spoke to me. I didn't know I had the Holy Spirit at the time. I was speaking in tongues but I didn't understand the person that was living inside of me was the Holy Spirit. The person said, "Write the judge and tell him what happened to you last night." I wasn't such a great writer but I got a dictionary and wrote the judge a letter. They laughed at me but I want you to know that the judge granted me a pardon and I was out of there in three months. That was the mercy of God. It was unheard of to only serve three months with three felonies under the belt. I look at it now as one month for the Father, one month for the Son, and one month for the Holy Spirit who took residence inside of me not too long ago. Yes, I knew God was real because He was the one who told me to write to the judge. Every day in that prison I communed with God. I was the happiest girl in the world because I had something I never had before. I had a relationship with the Lord.

As soon as I left prison, all hell broke loose. My husband did not like me being a Christian. Remember, I was that little girl who needed to be loved. That little girl who had such unmet needs. I had God on one side but, on the other side, my husband told me I couldn't go back to that church. They had service on Monday nights. I went back a couple of times but I would have to fight when I got home so I couldn't keep going there.

I ended up going back to the church I had always gone to and that I loved. It was okay to go there but it wasn't okay to go to Sweetness House. I joined the choir again but I was different. I didn't fit in but I went anyway. I want you to know that I slipped back into my old self. I started stealing again but not as bad as before because I had this new relationship. This relationship was so awesome and it wouldn't leave me alone. This relationship I had was always there.

I was still trying to find healing and deliverance so I went to church a lot. I felt safe in church because of the worship I would experience. I didn't go just anywhere. I chose churches that worshiped the Lord. I would go to churches if there was a speaker, but not just any speaker. I believe I was always being led.

Sadie Brunson

But I went to prison again.

The warden, who was my godmother, said if the Lord spared me that I would not make parole. But God told me I was going home. Favor and mercy followed me again. I went to the parole board at three months and they let me out. I was home for Thanksgiving. My godmother was so upset because she said my problem was that I didn't suffer. She said I needed to stay in prison and let my husband take care of me. She would let me go to church but she wouldn't let me work. That was my punishment. She didn't realize that's what I really needed, but maybe she did. Who knows? Maybe the Lord spoke to her.

You don't always know the plans God has for you but He does have a plan. When I went to prison, a woman named Joanne came to see me. She was another white woman. God used a lot of white women in my life. She came to the prison because she had read about me in the newspaper. She came with the love of salvation and we became very good friends. She was a very beautiful woman. She said to me, "I know a group of women with whom you need to be involved. The group is called Women Aglow and you're one of those type of women – you're Spirit-filled." She asked the warden if I could go and the warden said yes.

So I went to a Women Aglow meeting. The first time I went, I just knew everybody knew I was from prison but they didn't. It was just me feeling shame and guilt. There were at least 100 women there, maybe more. The whole ballroom was full.

What I loved about Women Aglow was the worship. Every time the Lord did something, there was worship. That's why I can say I'm a worshiper today. I don't like going to churches that don't worship. I will go because I'm the speaker, but there's something about the spirit of worship. This was back in the 70's and a lot of people were just learning how to worship but it's always been there. It was a part of my deliverance.

During worship I felt so much love because, in God, there is love. He inhabits the praises of His people (Psalm 22:3). You're telling Him you love Him and you're not asking for anything. I learned that in Women Aglow. I was only in that prison for three months but every month I was able to go to Women Aglow. When I got out, I joined them. I told them I had been in prison but they still accepted me. They didn't judge me. It seemed like they loved me more. I asked God why it is that when I'm with white people they love me so differently. They just accepted me for who I was when my own race criticized me. They would say I'm not saved or I'm not this or I'm not that. I was confused because I know I'm black but God used white people to draw me with love. God drew me with love.

I think He was trying to show me real love. He showed me that people loved me and I didn't have to steal or give them anything. I didn't have to do anything. I was a big tither at the church that I left. When I left that church, they didn't say we miss you; they said we miss your tithes. I told my mother that it really bothered me because I grew up in that church, but they didn't even miss me.

Then I would go to places like Women Aglow and they loved me. But I was always looking for more. I was hungry for God because He wanted me to have a closer relationship with Him. He wanted me to know I could trust Him. He began to tell me through others that He was going to deliver me. He also told me directly that He was going to deliver me. I had a hard time believing it because I thought it was going to happen quickly. You know how when you become pregnant, you're "delivered" in nine months? Well, I was waiting for nine months to go by thinking I would get delivered.

I eventually became Vice President of Women Aglow. Then I became President. I spoke at 13 chapters. God opened doors for me to speak. I was all over the place speaking – telling my story and giving my testimony. I was seeing women get set free and healed. Many times, after I finished, I felt like the enemy was telling me that I was nothing. I would feel so empty after I finished giving out but I would see how blessed they were and I would wonder when my turn would come.

I knew it wasn't me speaking but people would say, "Do you remember when you said this?" I didn't remember anything. The Lord just used me as a mouthpiece. He was speaking through me. I picked up a scripture in God's word, "It is no longer that I live but it is Christ that lives" (Gal. 2:20) and I began to see Him live through the ministry. I knew it wasn't me. It was awesome that He would use me in spite of myself but I couldn't explain it. He would tell me what to say all the time. When it was time for me to speak, I would just get up and say, "It is no longer that I live but it is Christ that lives."

God was living inside me even when I fell down. He still used me. That was so hard for me to understand. I used to tell Him, please don't make me stand up in front of those people because I don't feel worthy of this. I would just complain all the time, but the Lord kept pouring in the engagements. He just kept sending me to churches and I got better. I started feeling better about myself but I still didn't really know who I was. God hid that part of me from others. People prophesied a whole lot of stuff over me and God would tell me little things too but because of the fears, rejection and abandonment I hadn't dealt with, I lied to myself and believed the lie.

Because I hadn't dealt with my own issues, I couldn't receive truth from the Lord. I wasn't used to truth since my whole life was built on a lie. I don't know how God got in but He did. He got in there because He could commune with me and I wanted to commune with him. Then I would do something to disappoint him. I did it so much that I hated myself for it. It got to the point that I just told the Lord if He couldn't clean me, if He couldn't deliver me then I just wanted Him to take me home because I didn't want to go to hell. I used to talk to Him like that, and then I'd get a phone call asking me to come preach. He would never allow me to say no.

I would go and love God's people. I have a ministry of love and truth. I did this all by myself for a long time. Later on, God added people in my life to go with me, support me, and protect me in prayer. He added my friend, Donna, in my life and I thank Him for that.

When God first began to add people in my life, I really didn't want anyone to travel with me because I never felt worthy. To this day, I've never listened to any of my tapes from beginning to end. I listened to half of one tape once. I never wanted to listen to myself.

I didn't know how to love myself correctly because I lived in torment. I could get into God's presence, have a ball and stay there for a while but the next time an opportunity came, I would steal something. It was a horrible life for me. I thank Him because He gave me five years without stealing anything. I thought I had arrived...until I got married again.

When I went home that November, I went home with a warfare in my mouth – the blood of Jesus. Yes, I won and that's how I stayed free. I don't know how many years I stopped stealing. I would just say, "the blood of Jesus". My mother first taught me that but I heard it again on R. W. Shambock's radio station when I went to prison. I used to tell my mother I didn't want to listen to him. But God put me in a place where all I wanted to do was listen to him. The blood of Jesus was my warfare. When I was in Bible School we learned a whole lot of stuff but all you really have to do is believe in the blood of Jesus. If you put the blood on, Satan can't touch you. So that's what I did.

When I went back home, I was truly different. I was in the bathroom (which is one of the places where God speaks to me a lot) when the Lord said to me, "You can't compromise with the devil." I said, "What?" I really didn't know what that meant.

I was always kind of submissive so I asked my husband if I could go to church. When I say I was "kind of submissive", I mean I wasn't afraid to speak my mind but I wanted to be in agreement and keep peace with my husband. I had four children then and I wanted to keep the peace. Not only that, I changed. I stopped stealing. My husband didn't like the fact that I stopped stealing. He didn't like the new woman. He preferred the old woman. So that was a constant battle. Should I go back to my old self or should I stay with the new self? There was a power inside of me this time that made me able to stand. When I stood, I saw Jesus. He told me I couldn't compromise with the devil. I asked my husband if I could go to church Saturday night because this lady was coming to Mother Church of God in Christ and I just loved her. My mother had taken me to see her when I was a little girl and I wanted to see her again. He said, "If you go to church, you can't come back here anymore". The Lord had already told me I couldn't compromise with the devil so I went. I wasn't going to let him stop me.

I didn't go home that night. I slept at my beauty shop because I had two nice sofas there. When I finally went home, we didn't have a fistfight, but we had a fight. The next thing I knew, I could never go back to my house again. We ended up in court. The judge said we could both live in the house because I wanted a divorce. I couldn't compromise anymore. That's why I got a divorce. This divorce process was the ugliest thing I'd ever seen in my life. I had four closets full of clothes. My husband cut up every piece of my clothing. He took my furs and my diamonds and cut everything else up. He cut up the roof in the house so when it rained the floors buckled. The floors were beautiful. We had about five TVs and he put oil in all of them so they wouldn't work. He destroyed as much as he could to spite me.

In all of this excitement, the Lord showed me one thing, that my husband never put his hands on me. He thought that by destroying my goods it would stop me but it didn't. It only made me stronger. My next door neighbor was a police officer and he was a blessing to me. God really used him to minister to me during such an awkward time. The divorce was a very ugly battle. My ex-husband lied and told people that my best girlfriend and I were lovers. We had to live through that lie, however, I thank God for my girlfriend today. She's a preacher and she's going to preach all over the world. And so am I. The things we had to suffer in order to be free, just to serve God. But I made a choice not to let any man stop me from serving God anymore. I was determined.

My children had to sleep on the floor for the first time in their lives but God gave me double for my trouble. God gave me two beauty shops. He gave me an awesome condominium to live in until He gave me my home. My new house was so beautiful. It was the home I desired. He is such an awesome God. He showed up on my behalf and blessed me. He gave me buildings and properties in that season. I came to a place in God where I wasn't going to let any husband dictate to me anymore because I found out that it's not about him but it's about God. I didn't even realize the strength I had. During those three months in prison when I was able to go to Women Aglow meetings, feast on the word of God and look at PTL (Praise The Lord) on TV everyday, I'd gotten stronger in the Lord. I didn't even know it until I got into a situation that tested me. I stood for the first time. The insecure little girl finally stood up in a power that I knew wasn't me.

I went through that divorce and was humiliated in court. One of my girlfriends, Helen, worked in the court building. Later on I met her at Victory Christian Fellowship. She told me how it seemed like my life was being destroyed when that man got up and said I was a lesbian and he wanted to take the children away from me. But the Lord worked that out for me too. A few church people believed it because they'll believe anything. Some of them want to believe the worst about others anyway because it keeps their own shortcomings out of the limelight. They look for reasons not to like you. I told you I found out about real people when I went to prison. They were real people with real pain and real issues. Many of them went to church and cried out to God to help them to stop stealing, and to stop being a whoremonger. They didn't care who heard them. I heard people cry out to God in prison. They wanted God to help them to love their kids and to help them to be a better wife and help them not to abuse their children. I heard those kinds of things and I said, "Lord, thank you." The Lord was working on me and I finally passed the test. Hallelujah!

Sadie Brunson

Chapter 6
Marriage #3

But guess what? I still had unmet needs. I still lived in that rejected body. But that didn't stop me from getting married again right away. Oh, and guess what else? I received a prophecy. The prophecy was that I was going to meet somebody special when I went into the prisons to speak and that I was going to marry him. That's exactly what happened.

When I went to the prison to speak, I met this guy there who was an inmate and I married him. He was so nice; well, at least he seemed nice. The chaplain introduced me to him just like the prophecy said. He had life in prison but I believed him when he said he didn't do it. I prayed and fasted for him and, believe it or not, God set him free.

Throughout our marriage, we were able to sponsor 11 trips to PTL for other people to get saved. My beauty shops grew by leaps and bounds like never before. I had 17 operators working at the shops and money was coming from everywhere. I had a shop in Wilmington and one in Dover. I made so much money I didn't even have time to count it. However, the things I went through in our marriage were not what I'd expected to happen.

I was so rejected in this marriage. I failed God again. I kept attracting my addiction. I was a rejected person so I kept attracting who I was. I had such a need to be loved. The man I married was a "meek sneak". My daughter Tracy gave him that name because he did everything you would ask him to do but, on the other side, he would sneak out of the house to be with other women. Then he would come home like he did nothing wrong. He would also sneak out of the house to get high. When he began to lose weight, I began to pray and ask God what the problem was. The Lord told me that my husband was using coke. I told my girlfriend what God told me. Neither of us used drugs so we didn't know what coke was. I would find these little pipes in the car and I used to say, "these are the cutest little pipes." I thought they were for smoking cigarettes or tobacco. I didn't know any better. He was smoking crack and I had no idea until the car was repossessed.

That's how naive I was. I had no clue he was doing this behind my back. I was so scared. I didn't know what to do. So how did I respond? I went back to my old self and got into a lot of trouble. I got into so much trouble that I knew this was the end for me because I had about 18 felonies. That's total life in prison. So here I get arrested again and the Holy Spirit comes in and tells me that He is going to cover me. And guess what? They didn't lock me up. They just talked to me, had me sign a release form and let me go home.

The Lord told me to call my spiritual daughter, Faye. She came to pick me up because I couldn't drive home. I was so amazed how God gave me mercy…again. As wrong as I was, He came with mercy. He didn't come with judgment. But rather, He hid me. I told Faye what God had said.

Knowing that this was the biggest case I'd ever had, I just knew it would be in the newspaper but, bless God, it wasn't. When I think about the mercy of God, I think about David because his family rejected him. His wife and his son rejected him but he still had the heart of God. It seems so undeserved but I would think about him and how God showed him so much mercy. Not that I haven't reaped for many of the things I've done, but one thing I understand, even through my rejection, is that God displayed His mercy and love towards me (Romans 5:8).

This happened on the weekend of my daughter's debutante ball. I'll never forget it because I had to act as though nothing was wrong. I was all dressed up in a beautiful gown. My husband and I were walking around at the ball. I'm sure he was disappointed in me because I was disappointed in myself. I was smiling and crying at the same time. I looked up and there was my lawyer at the ball. I danced with him and then took him outside and told him what happened. He said, "Oh my God, how am I going to get you out of this? You need another lawyer." He got me the best lawyer there was and it cost me a lot of money. But when I got to court, they squashed the case.

God had already promised He was going to cover me. That's all He told me. Faye and I prayed in her grandmother's bathroom. We didn't want her grandmother to know what we were saying, so we would steal away to pray. We were in the bathroom and the Holy Spirit closed the door. We knew He was there so we stopped praying. It seemed strange but He began to speak through Faye. He told her to tell me that my children were going to rise up and call me blessed. It came out of her mouth. It was so much like God. I never thought my kids would ever call me blessed because I lived a double life.

I went through another divorce. My daughter, Nikki was in college. My girls were big kids then. Michael wasn't that old, maybe seven or eight. I'm not really sure. But I was really rooted and grounded in church more so than anything.

Nikki had a hard time in college financially because I was divorced then. Every time I got divorced, I would lose. She was about to graduate. That was all that mattered to me. I remember her graduation. I was so tired trying to make it. Trying to make sure she had everything she needed. As I said earlier, I wasn't stealing that much. In fact, I went for years without stealing at all. I thought I was delivered but I wasn't.

My daughter's graduation was so beautiful. I was able to take her and her friends to a beautiful hotel. I also took Nikki and her friends out to her favorite restaurant. My car had broken down so I got a brand new Cadillac to take her to graduation in. I wanted her to have the best. I always wanted my children to have the best. I gave what I had.

At the graduation ceremony, I fell asleep. Jesse Jackson was the speaker. I heard some of it but I was so tired of Sadie. I was tired of being so many things just trying to make it all happen. I was so much into reasoning. I always had to have plan A and plan B for everything. If this didn't work, then that would work. I didn't allow God be Lord over my life. I was so busy trying to make things right but to no avail.

My children worked for me in the beauty shop. They were raised in the beauty shop. I would cook and bring their food to the beauty shop. They would do their homework in the beauty shop. They were awesome kids. God knew I couldn't handle it if they were horrible. They helped me with Michael. They helped me keep the house clean. I had the kind of husband where you had no other choice but to keep everything clean. They were very disciplined. As they grew up I found out that they were all different. You know how you think your kids are like you and you tell them that. Well, I found out that they did everything in their power not to be like me. Working with them was a challenge but it was a good challenge. I could depend on them. They became very good operators. They could really do hair.

Chapter 7

Overcoming Abusiveness

I was an abusive mother. In this relationship with God, I found out I had issues. One of the first issues God showed me was that I was abusive. He showed me how I hollered and screamed at my children all the time. He told me to take this class on Abusive Mothers. That was back when I was in my early 30's. There were all kinds of women in this class and they were reaching out for help. I listened to them because you don't see yourself until you see others. They would get up and tell what they did. I was very prideful because my kids had all the material things and they never knew what it was not to have. They went to the best of schools, lived in the nicest homes and had the best toys. They had the best of everything; they just didn't have their mother. I was in my own little world. The enemy had taken my mind.

I was a functioning mother but I was always driven by my addiction. I had very little patience. I wanted everything to be perfect. I saw myself as ugly, miserable and living two lives. I didn't want them to be like the bad side of me because it was so hard to live those two lives.

The anger would come out. I screamed at my youngest daughter the most. I really loved her but, before she was born, I remembered praying and telling God I didn't want another child. I had just had Nikki and, right afterwards, I was pregnant with Marlene. I didn't want to have another child because I was so messed up. How could I bring another child into the world when my life was in such turmoil? She didn't deserve the hell I took her through as a little girl.

As I'm thinking about this, I want to say to hurting women, please get help before you have a child. They don't deserve any of the abuse or rejection you would inflict on them because of selfishness. I thank God for forgiving me for hurting my little girls. I didn't want to hurt them. I wanted to protect them. I didn't want them to be molested like I was.

God showed me that my father abandoned me but I didn't understand that's what was driving me. I wanted the love of a father so much. It damaged me so badly that I desperately wanted my kids to have a father. I didn't want them to be without. I wanted them to have a father to speak over their lives and love them, which was the very thing I missed. The only father figure I had was my stepfather and he molested me.

I believe with all of my heart that every man I married was good to my kids. They had their issues but they tried to be good fathers, especially my third husband. He was very disciplined but he instilled good things in my kids. We went through a lot of things but he still tried to be a good father to them and I thank God for that.

The damage was already done to my daughters – the hollering, the screaming, and the cursing – all because of my pain. Of course, that was no excuse. When God shined the flashlight on my wounds, I had to come clean. That was the beginning of some form of deliverance in my life. God told me the damage had already been done but I realized that time always brings healing.

Chapter 8
Running Away Didn't Help

As the journey goes on, I went back to Victory Christian Fellowship. When I first left Victory, I had gone to a Baptist church called St. Daniels. God didn't tell me where to go so I just went to St. Daniels because there were a lot of mature, sophisticated women and men of God. They were so different from anyone I'd ever been around. They had such class but they still loved me. I went to the New Beginners classes and I loved it. They taught me about the Holy Spirit and so many other awesome things about God. Most of all, they taught me about love and they practiced that by demonstrating it to me. My children really didn't like it there at first but they went with me anyway.

One day, Bishop Roy Davis walked up to me and said, "I believe God has more for you. I believe you should seek Him for a church because you speak in tongues." I didn't even know that he knew I spoke in tongues. I always spoke in tongues quietly and I always raised my hands up to God. I was the only one in the church who did that.

I started seeking the Lord for a church. God didn't answer right away so I followed a girlfriend to another church which was Pentecostal. They shouted and jumped all over the building. They did what I called the "hoochie koochie" on people. They would wave their hands all up and down over people but it was spooky. I had never seen people do the "hoochie koochie" on people before. One Sunday I brought a male friend who was an ex-pimp to church with me because he wanted to be saved. The women got him up to the altar and did the "hoochie koochie" on his body. I was so devastated that I went up there and got him. I said, "Get your hands off of him." They were waving their hands up and down his body and speaking in tongues. He was ready to jump out of his skin so I went to rescue him. He and I laugh about that a lot.

I still ended up joining that church because I wanted to be in a church. I wanted to join the choir but the pastor told me I couldn't sing on the choir because I wore lipstick. I knew I had missed God on this. When I got saved, I had lipstick on and He accepted me as I was. He didn't say I couldn't come into His kingdom because I was wearing lipstick and jewelry. I liked the people but I had to leave.

The Lord spoke to me and said, "Go back to Victory Christian Fellowship." And I said, "Where is it?" I just drove around looking for it because I knew they had moved somewhere in Newport. It took me about three days to find it. The first Sunday I went, there was a guest speaker named Bishop Benson Idahosa. Prior to this, a prophet had told me I was going to go to Bible school. I had never finished high school but she told me I wouldn't be happy until I did the things God was calling me to do. That was in my spirit.

When I went to church that morning, there was so much love there. It was where I belonged because they worshiped the Lord. The Klaxtons were over the worship team and my friend Helen was there. It was so marvelous. When I lifted my hands to God, there was such a release of His presence. He just took over. He ministered to me and loved on me. I didn't know how hungry I was for the Lord. I was divorced at that time so I didn't have anybody controlling me. I felt like I was in heaven and the presence of the Lord was there.

I went back that night and Bishop Idahosa spoke again. We were just starting a Bible school and it was our first year. He asked anyone that didn't have the money to pay for Bible school to come up front and stand on one side. I went up there, with my hurting self. I was hurting and so confused but I was hungry inside. There was an emptiness inside of me that needed to be filled. I had so many issues but there was a God who never left me nor forsook me. He pulled me out of my chair and I obeyed Him.

When our Bishop said come, I stood in that line. There was another group, a big group, who had money. But there was a group of us that didn't have the money. A member in the church, a doctor's wife, tapped me on the shoulder. She said, "God told me to pay your way. Go sit down." After service she said, "Come tomorrow and I'll meet you at registration." She paid my way to go to Bible school. The first year of Bible school I didn't take any tests. I just sat there and absorbed the Word because I was desperate to be loved.

God always made a way for me and I've always had favor with God. He told me that back in 1972 when He saved me. There were many times in my life when I knew I didn't deserve His favor, but I wouldn't back up.

Right before going to Victory, I had a lot of outstanding charges that I had run from when I lived in Atlanta, GA for a year. I knew they would never come to Delaware to get me for those charges. I was trying to run from my troubles and I was trying to run from Sadie. I thought if I left town and changed addresses I would change.

While I was in Atlanta, I found a great church to go to called St. Matthews. I had never seen so many people fit into a church. I loved that church. The pastor was very charismatic and he was full of the Spirit. His church was small, but not small. There were so many people who came. He spoke right into my life every Sunday but I was still addicted. I had a wonderful job in Atlanta but I began stealing again. That same demon was there all the time.

We had a lot of material things. We lived in a beautiful neighborhood and we had a beautiful apartment with three bedrooms and a fireplace. And I still had a home and business back in Wilmington.

When I was scheduled to go to court in Atlanta, I just packed up everything and went back to Delaware because I hadn't sold my house. I kept my house and my beauty shop in Wilmington. My operators ran the shop just as if I was there. When I worked in Atlanta, my children were in school there. My eldest daughter was 15. She also worked in Atlanta; I think it was her first job. But I packed up everything and went back home. I was glad to go back home because I didn't really like Atlanta since I didn't fit in. What I saw was a bunch of people who were phony and I don't like phony people. When I went to prison and when I went to girls' school, I met real people who had real issues. God would always show up for someone who was real. It seemed like I always attracted phony people because, as much as I liked to think I was real, I was phony. And I always attracted what I was. I attracted people who were addicted, materialistic and who said one thing but did another. I always attracted people like that. Why not? Look who I was. Who was I trying to fool?

One day, out of the blue, the presence of the Lord spoke to me and said, "Call Atlanta and deal with that situation." I called Atlanta and they said they would come get me. I was at the point where I wasn't afraid to face it because I wanted to be healed. I wanted to be real and I wanted a different life. So I dealt with it. The Atlanta authorities came to pick me up.

Mercy Rewrote My Life

I had to go to the women's prison in Delaware overnight when I turned myself in. The next morning, Atlanta's officers picked me up. Thankfully, the bailiff told them not to handcuff me. They put me on a plane and flew me first class. They took me to court and the judge held me over. I had to go to prison because I couldn't make bail. Of course, I wasn't expecting that. I was sent to the worst prison I'd ever been to in my life. There were roaches everywhere and I was afraid of roaches. There were lesbians everywhere. I didn't take my clothes off nor did I shower or bathe.

They had a church service that first night so I went. At the service, there was a group of white women who came and taught on the 91st Psalm. That scripture came alive to me right then – that He would hide me in the shadow of the Most High God. I cried and cried and cried because I was so ashamed and because I felt like I always let God down.

The girls in prison thought I was a schoolteacher because I was so well dressed. I was able to call my mother who now, along with my husband, was left to take care of the kids. My mother spoke a word over my life. She said, "Sadie, stop crying. You need God's mercy now." My mother spoke such faith to me that I took hold of it. I took hold of her faith.

God used a lesbian at that prison to tell me to take my clothes off, take a shower and brush my teeth. She told me that she would protect me. She asked if I had seen my face. There were 19 pimples on my face. I looked like a monster. This girl told me, "God is going to set you free because there's something different about you."

I asked her why she was there. She told me she was sentenced to life because she had killed her lover and was just waiting to go to the prison where she was going to serve her time. I was so afraid of that woman but God used her to be kind to me and to show me favor. I never knew who God would use to help me.

My mother was powerful. She was very strong and she took authority over my tears. She took authority over that spirit for me and spoke life to me. I received that life when I grabbed hold to the word mercy and I began to speak, "God have mercy, God have mercy." When I finished speaking that word, I began to feel the mercy of God. It allowed me to take a shower and to change my clothes. I was able to go to sleep peacefully. I was afraid that the roaches would crawl in my ears but God protected me. He showed such mercy to me.

When I went to court the judge had already decided he was going to give me three years. I had the best lawyer but my record was so bad. Back home in Delaware, the baptist church I used to go to had taken an offering and sent three deacons to stand with me on the day I went to court. These were three men I knew had issues but God chose to send those three men. All three of them were Masons and so was the judge. The judge asked the three men to come to his chambers. He had already told my lawyer how much time he was going to give me. But when he came back into the courtroom and began to sentence me he said, "I sentence you to" and stopped. Then he turned around in the chair and said, "Get out of Atlanta. I'm going to give you a year's probation. You can't come back to Atlanta for a year." The Lord said, "Mercy". He gave me mercy and I got out. I cried and cried and said thank you.

Everyone in the courtroom was saying, "Wow, that's a miracle!" The judge changed his mind and I knew it was God who worked on him. I thank the Lord today for the mercy of God because it was His mercy that rewrote my life.

Sadie Brunson

Chapter 9

God Used Me Anyway

I went home and went back to Victory Christian Fellowship. I became very close to Pastor Faye and was able to share some things about my life with her. She was very open with me and shared some things about her life too. That's the first time I could truly say that I shared with a pastor who received me without judging me. I loved her for that. I loved Pastors Faye and Gary for the truth. God gave me a close relationship with them.

I went to Bible school and I remember filling out applications and having to say I was on probation. They never judged me. I didn't care that they used it as a testimony. I did a lot of wonderful things while I was there. I got to go into a lot of churches.

During the time I was in Bible school, I attended a hairdresser's convention right after I had divorced my third husband. I was with a guy who was a very good friend of mine. He was a real sharp hairdresser who loved the Lord. He told me about a pastor named Beverly "Bam" Crawford. We called her Bam Bam. He said you've got to come to New York to see her. I told him my daughter was doing a recording that weekend and I had to be with her. He said, "Go hear your daughter, get a late train out and I'll meet you."

I finally arrived in New York. My friend was a new member at this church, Redeeming Christian Love. He wore $1200 shoes. Back then, we were all that and then some. We had so many masks on and we were so materialistic. We made a lot of money in the beauty industry so we could buy anything we wanted. That day it rained and he had parking lot duty. It was the funniest thing because his shoes got all messed up outside while I got to go into the service to hear Beverly "Bam" Crawford. When I heard her, I thought I was going to lose my mind. I said, "Oh my God." I had never been in a church like Redeeming Christian Love before. I felt like I was in heaven. She was the prettiest pastor's wife I'd ever seen and she was also a pastor. Sara and Clint Arterback were so beautiful. They were so loving.

And the worship! I was just so in love. When she got up to speak, I had never heard anybody speak truth like she did. Everybody talks about what happened in the Bible but this woman talked about what God had done for her. She talked about being a prostitute and so many other things. I said to myself, "What? Church people tell stuff like that?" It just blew me away. God said, "This is who you are because you will tell on the devil. You will expose what he's done to you." But first He let me see someone who was already exposing the enemy and I bought every tape she had.

I went all over the place to hear her speak. I went to California, Atlanta, Florida, New Jersey and back. I went to New York to hear her several times. Every time I saw her, it seemed like God did something in me. It was just an awesome time with God. I traveled to every conference there was because I wanted deliverance and I wanted to be healed. I saw Bishop Weeks everywhere I would go because I always went to pastor and leadership sessions.

One time, I took a group of women with me to Ernestine Reems' conference in California called "Women of Color". It was so awesome. I saw Bishop Weeks there too. I didn't know him then but I knew we were from the same town so we would always speak to each other.

Mercy Rewrote My Life

I took a lot of white women with me to this conference. When I would get something from God, I wanted everyone else to get it too. I would spend my money just so that I could sow into others' deliverance and healing. I wanted everybody to be healed. I wanted to give away what God was giving me. I couldn't explain it so I'd just say come, go with me.

I think I took about 15 people with me that time. For some of them it was their first time on a plane. God made a way for everyone to have their own room. At that conference, every speaker on the platform spoke a word over me. They spoke things that were so great. I didn't know how I could ever achieve those things because I didn't have any education and I had no desire to go back to school. I did go back a couple of times but I couldn't focus. The Lord would say I didn't tell you to do this and I would leave. I would ask myself, "How could God ever want to use me like these people were saying?"

One lady behind me said, "You're going to be a millionaire." I'd heard that about four or five times at that conference. One woman said, "I'm already a millionaire and I know one when I see one." I was so blessed at that conference. I felt so special. I thought, maybe I am a good girl; perhaps I am somebody. But I had such low self-esteem that I didn't feel worthy of any of it. I was just bouncing thoughts around.

Ernestine Reems got up and asked who was the lady who brought all these white women? I stood up and they clapped. All the women were coming over to me and saying how nice it was. I just said, "They're my friends. We go to church together and we're in Women Aglow together. I wanted them to come because the speakers are so awesome." God used these speakers to speak into my life. This was years ago in the late eighties and early nineties. It's just awesome how God prepares you with prophetic words because He knows that one day it's going to happen.

I had a wonderful time at that conference and I went home a changed woman. Beverly "Bam" Crawford was so good. She was the highlight of that conference for me. She had a seminar dealing with pastors' wives. And, of course, if Beverly taught it, I went. I'd never seen pastors' wives get real. They were falling out on the floor crying. I remember looking at them and wondering what was wrong with them? Why wouldn't they just admit they were hurting? Why wouldn't they admit that they don't like people? Why wouldn't they admit they're not called to be what "people" say they're called to be? They were going crazy in that room. I had gotten to the point where I could be honest about my pain. I was at a point where I didn't have to tell people "I'm blessed" if I felt miserable. I didn't understand why they had to be phony. Who were they really trying to impress?

I'd gotten to that place by being around Beverly because I was seeing her set them free. I saw how they were all dressed up and wouldn't even speak to people unless you went to their church. It was just so ironic how I wanted the Lord to do something to help them. Who needed more help than me? But I knew I loved people and I was never standoffish. I never thought I was better than anybody else no matter what I had. I always knew it was God who kept me and that I needed Jesus everyday. I knew I had the issue of stealing. I knew my father, who left us and never wanted to see us again, had abandoned me. I knew a Baptist preacher had molested me. And, most of all, I knew I had scars. Why would I pretend nothing was wrong? How could I act like every day was a good day? I wasn't there yet. I learned to tell people the truth. Every time I told truth, I saw the hand of God. I found out that God loves truth. If you just get up and say, Lord, I'm blessed or thank you because I've got it all together, God couldn't do anything with that. What could He do?

I was a little bit different but those were the things I believed because He always showed up in my life with grace and mercy. Anytime I asked Him for grace to love somebody or to forgive them, it was easy.

One thing I can say about Beverly "Bam" Crawford is that when she got up, God got up. The truth that came out of her mouth was awesome. Truth will convict and it will bring people to their knees. That's what I saw in that conference in 1990 and I'll never forget it. It was such a long time ago as I was on my journey of finding deliverance but she is one of the greatest deliverance ministers I've ever met in my life. I thank the Lord for her.

On my journey of healing, the Lord allowed me to go to a lot of places. I've been to Africa, Paris, Europe, Israel and Holland. I've been to so many places I can't even remember all of them. I've been searching for healing.

God showed me myself in Israel as people came up to me and ministered. They told me that I was a queen and that I had one of the greatest Jewish names, Sadie. They told me how beautiful it was. I've always hated my name because it was always in the newspaper whenever I was arrested. It represented the bad and that's how I saw myself, bad little Sadie Shy. After I went to Israel, I started to like my name because somebody showed me the other side of it and the meaning of it. It meant so much more to me then. They gave me so many gifts when I went to Israel that I had to buy a suitcase for them. They took pictures of me and told me I was beautiful.

I was 40 years old. It's amazing how God allowed me to be loved in a country I didn't know anything about. In Europe and Russia, they loved me too. They took pictures of me and told me I was the most beautiful black woman they had ever seen. I was smiling but I smiled all the time anyway. My smile drew people to me even though I was still living in a rejected body. Not only was I rejected, but the Lord also told me I had the root of rejection. After walking with the Lord for a while, I became more and more open with people.

When I was going to Bible school, Reverend Gif who is a pastor now, was in school with me. He used to tell me I was so blessed. I used to frown when he said that and tell him to leave me alone because my past and my pain wouldn't let me receive what God had for me.

I was still on this journey looking for deliverance and healing.

Chapter 10
The House That Rejection Built

I want to talk a little bit about rejection and how we attract it.
I want to talk a little bit about the house that rejection built.
I was at a point where I even rejected myself. I allowed satan
to build a house for me that made me feel anything but at
home. I felt unworthy and worthless. I wished I'd never
been born. Then I felt inferior, guilty, hurt, wounded, and in
pain. I felt like I had a generational curse that handicapped
my mind wouldn't let me trust anyone because I'd been
betrayed, abandoned and neglected. This is how I felt for
many years even though God's hand was on me. The root of
rejection produced so much pain. Satan took advantage of
my pain and used it to build his house. He used materials
from my past, which included a rejection personality. I was in
a rut of confusion. How could God love me when I didn't
love myself?

Rejection is one of the biggest hindrances to spiritual maturity
in the body of Christ today. It is amazing to see how many
people respond to life through hurts, wounds and scars from
the past. Our prayer should be that we might be able to
understand the root of rejection and how to achieve freedom
from this stronghold that has us bound. We will spend time
pulling apart the different elements of rejection so we can all
understand why we feel and act the way we do.

I had to tell myself that I was a fearful person and that I
feared the opinions of people. I was always trying to fit in but
never really felt like I belonged. I thought good things
belonged to everyone but me. I was seeking the attention and
approval of others. Oh how I wanted to be delivered. Every
time I filled out my tithing envelope I wrote, "Lord, thank

you for healing me." It took God to show me how to tear down the things satan had built in my life.

We must be taught how to separate feelings from truth. Rejection wants to tell us who we are. It gives us an identity of low self-esteem through flesh working rather than the identity God has provided for us in Christ. Flesh will attempt to achieve self-worth by works; it lies to us. It tells us we're worthless to ourselves and to others. We must learn to identify the feelings of rejection and understand the source so we can submit to the truth of the word of God. The rejection went on but I thank God again for His mercy, which was so awesome.

Rejection is like internal walls that keep even God's love from getting through. Rejection fills us with unworthy thoughts. It gets us to dwell on the unworthiness in ourselves. The house the enemy builds stacks a case against us and makes us feel trapped between a rock and a hard place.

When we pray, we must be ready to tear down the strongholds and declare that we are worthy. If we don't, we will never be able to be happy in Jesus. We will lie to ourselves. All of us have insecurities, no matter who we pretend to be.

Chapter 11

Unfailing Love

I took some time out. The Lord told me not to look at TV so I didn't look at TV for about two years. I got into a Bible school and became a real good student. I still had a lot of anger, mainly because I was angry with myself. I was generally nice to people though, unless they did something really bad to me. Sometimes I realized it wasn't worth it to deal with them because they were also hurting. God gave me a lot of wisdom to be able to look at people and see the goodness in them and the pain. I didn't have to hurt them back. Even when my husband was leaving, he turned around and said, "I've never had anybody who loves me like you do." I made sure he got all his stuff. I didn't care how badly I was hurting; I wanted him to be ok too. I always had a heart for people to be happy and healed. I didn't want to hurt anybody anymore.

I was able to travel all over the world for about seven years. I went somewhere almost every month. I was always going somewhere trying to get healed and spending a lot of money on what I believed. I spent a lot of money seeking the kingdom, trying to find Jesus. All I had was a heavenly Father who I knew loved me. I wanted to meet some people who were really healed and could tell their story. Bev was probably the only one that I heard who really told her story. She didn't cut any corners. I used to listen to her tapes over and over again to build myself up.

I completed Bible school. I went to early morning prayer every morning at 5:30 a.m. for three years without missing a morning. I didn't go because it was religious; I went because I needed it. I went because I needed God like I never needed Him before. I was desperate for God and wanted to love and obey Him. I knew He loved me but I didn't know how to love Him or be faithful to Him. I wanted to learn how to do that.

I went to a couple of Narcotics Anonymous (NA) meetings because they were able to talk about their feelings. In church, I couldn't raise my hand to ask a question or interrupt the flow. So I needed a place to go where I could have two-way communication. At NA, I could communicate too. I went to Alcoholics Anonymous also, because I could speak freely. I could say I had a good day or I could say I failed and not feel like I was being judged.

God began to minister to me and tell me who I was. He would write it on the wall at Victory as I was sitting in service. It was a big church and I'd be worshiping and would see His hand writing on the wall. He would tell me He was going to heal me. That gave me hope because He said, "I'm going to heal you and then use you as a healer to set the captives free." I kept asking God, "When are you going to heal me?" I would cry all the time. I wanted to be healed so desperately.

I didn't know anything but pain all my life. I woke up in the morning and it was heartache. I would close my eyes at night and it was heartache. I knew nothing but pain. What a miserable life I had! Then God would come in and He would bless me. He would show love to me. He would let me enter into His Spirit. He endowed me with His presence and with His love. I could come home and be okay for a couple of days or weeks or years. Then I would fall again. I had a hard time on my journey but I never quit. No matter how dark it was, I never got off the journey because He told me He was going to heal me. He used many other people to tell me the same thing.

At times, I would think I was healed because I would do well for years and be successful for years. I would go into churches and people would be blessed and touched by God. They'd cry and write to me and send me offerings. I thought I was ok because people wanted to be around me. They would call me and ask for advice. The Holy Spirit used me to heal marriages but my marriages were never healed. He also used me to stop divorces and women would come to me for Godly wisdom.

I can remember taking a class on submitting to your husband. My husband said to me, "You don't have to take that class; I love you the way you are." But I wanted to take the class anyway. I took several classes on how to be a good wife. I wanted to be a good wife and a good mother. And I wanted to be set free from stealing because, then, I would be delivered.

Everything about God is in His time, not when we want it. He told us to seek the kingdom first, then all of these other things shall be added (Matthew 6:33). But I was still seeking other stuff too. The most amazing thing happened to me after I went to all the wrong places to be healed. It was graduation day at Victory (it was also Mother's Day). The Lord spoke to me and said, "I want you to leave here because I'm ready to heal you". I was very excited about being healed but I didn't want to leave Victory. Where else could I go that would be as great as Victory? The church that was worth the drive and where they told you details. The church where God put two people together who were divorced and were willing to be spiritually naked and not ashamed. Where else could I go where the people were transparent? I felt so safe there and God used me there. I didn't do a lot of changing when I was at Victory though. Nor was I able to receive. But I was always able and ready to give.

Sadie Brunson

When I left Victory, I went on a journey. There were times I didn't really know where to go. I ended up in a church in Ocean City (in the Berlin area) with this great pastor and wife. I went there for two years and God used me to preach often. I didn't even know where I was half the time because He used me so much. When I would go out to speak, people would fill the place to hear me. They would receive the words God gave me to speak and would be delivered and set free from bondage. They would call me on the phone and say, you said this or you did this or God really used you. It was so amazing to me how the power of God used me. They would tell me all these great things and I realized what it meant to be a vessel of God.

On my journey to find love, God used another white lady. Her name was Greta. She was an awesome prophet who spoke into my life. It looked like a thousand people were in the room and she picked me out. I wasn't even in the service yet; I was just coming through the door. She said, "The woman who just walked in, come quickly." She had been in the middle of dismissing the service so everyone was standing up. I couldn't figure out how she even saw me. She said, "God's going to use you and you're going to be able to tell people what's on their hearts. You're going to hear God's heart. He is going to trust you with His heart. You're going to have to go through a few things now but you're going to make it." She had every one of those women point their hands towards me as she prayed.

After that was over, I felt so alone and ashamed. The women were saying, "Girl, did you hear that prophecy?" I wasn't thinking about the prophecy. I was thinking about my struggles because I always knew God could take care of His business. He'd already demonstrated His power in my dirty vessel. I knew I wanted to be free of the yokes. I needed someone to minister to me who had also walked in rejection. So I began seeking the Lord that Greta would give me another prophecy. And she did. She selected me and a woman named Sarah. She gave us what seemed like a harsh prophecy but it was really a great prophecy. She said, "I'm going to tell you two women something. God is giving you the power to endure like good soldiers." She said to me, "What God has for you is so big; it's like an ark and God's going to send them two by two. In order for them to be delivered and to be healed, they're going to have to come to this ark. They're going to come." She also said, "God is going to use you to speak to people that you don't even think would listen to you." I began to collect arks because I didn't understand the prophecy. Nor did I understand that I was being raised up to be a deliverer.

I ended up in the men's prison teaching for eight years. The warden would let me stay past the time limit. Sometimes I would go and stay for three hours. God was teaching me how to love men and teaching me how they were hurting. He was teaching me that they were little boys inside, just like my inner little girl that needed to be healed, not persecuted. I began to pray and ask God to please forgive me for hurting men. I asked Him to show me how to love them correctly and God began to show me. They used to break when I'd go there. They'd talk about being molested. And I would say, "God, they've been through this too." They used to break when I talked about how they were abandoned and how they were dropped. How people who were supposed to take care of them molested them. I would talk about those things and I actually saw Jesus use me to bring freedom to those men.

I would walk out of there weeping so badly that the guards would ask me if the men did anything to offend me. I couldn't cry in there, but when I walked out, I couldn't wait to cry because I could feel their pain and their love. They were like scared little children and I could relate to that because I was a fearful woman trapped in a child's pain. I began to teach about the little boy that needed to be healed. They could relate to me because I said my little girl is on a journey of healing too. They would be so blessed by me coming. I used to tell God I didn't understand why they received me so well.

God began to build my confidence in speaking. I would open my mouth to speak and He'd use me. I was okay with that because I knew it wasn't me who was speaking. It was Christ who was speaking through me. I could never take the credit or the glory because I knew it wasn't me. It kept me humble and looking towards Jesus. I knew He would show up for His people in spite of me because it was about God wanting to use me. He promised that He would set me free and heal me.

While I was at Victory, Pastor Gary taught a class on spiritual warfare. I had attended 16 classes up to that point. In the 17th class, Pastor Gary taught on a topic that caught my attention. The rest of the topics didn't mean that much to me even though it was good truth. But in class 17, he talked about the battle in the mind. That was the part that meant so much to me. It let me know that the enemy was in my mind. It was the things I thought. It was in that class that I learned how to tear down imaginations. It was what I thought that caused me problems. On days when I was weak, I would let the enemy use my thoughts and I would find myself acting out those thoughts. It was so easy to go back to old thought patterns because they were so familiar.

I knew a lot of people who struggled with drugs and struggled with male or female issues. They'd do well for a while, but until they were totally set free, they'd all travel back in their minds and find themselves in the old waste places. They hadn't allowed God to fill those places. That's why they'd find themselves doing the same old things over and over again.

We feel like we need to hide our unmet needs. We do it so well. The fear of feeling unloved is probably the greatest source of insecurity, whether or not we can be honest with ourselves. God uses "unfailing love" 32 times in His word and not one of them is in reference to any other love than Himself. But we look for others to meet those needs. God has the advantage because He created us. God can make us any way He wants us. He is not willing to see anyone perish. Since the only way we can have eternal life is through receiving Him, why don't we receive Him?

That was one of my biggest problems because I thought I had to work for it. I thought I had to earn it because I was so independent. I felt as though I needed to prove something. But I found out all I had to do was receive. I didn't have to do anything except receive. He had to teach me that I couldn't beat Him giving. A friend of mine named Kay told me the same thing one day when I was feeling down in my spirit. She said, "Sadie, you can't beat God giving no matter how hard you try." My grandmother Sadie taught me those words too and she made me learn that song.

She told me, when I was 12 years old, to always pay God by giving Him the tithe. From the age of 12 years old, I always gave my tithes. My tithes used to be big. I was the type of person who wanted to give a big tithe. I didn't want to give just $10 or $20; that seemed like nothing to me. I always wanted to give large amounts. Sometimes I would give $100 or $200 because I just loved to give. He made a way for me to give big tithes. I thought I had big things in heaven stored up for me because I always gave big. I purposed in my heart to give to God because I knew it was Him who told me to be a hairdresser. So I always gave God the tithe on my earnings and I always gave a lot in offerings. I also learned how to be a blessing to people on a weekly basis. I looked for people to give to because I wanted to be healed and delivered. I wanted God to always give to me.

I would buy clothes and pretend somebody gave them to me so I could give them away. I would buy pampers for babies because I knew the mommies didn't have money to buy them. I would walk down the street just to find people to bless with $10 or $20. I would also feed them because I was a giver. I enjoyed giving because God gave me more than enough. I had accounts at the State Store and the hoagie store for people who were homeless so I could send them there to be fed. Since I've always had more than enough, I was never selfish in giving. I always knew He would take care of me. There was something in me that knew that. When I was in my worst situation with all those felonies, God said, "I'm going to hide you." How could you tell the church that when they thought you had to pay for everything? They made you feel you had to pay.

But God told me one day, "I paid it all and I died for sinners. I loved and cared for you when I died for you. I gave my best for you and one day you will give me your best." God is so awesome!

The fear of feeling unloved is probably our greatest source of insecurity. God alone can provide unfailing love. From anyone else, it is fruitless. When you think someone else is going to love you unfailingly, your life is miserable, disappointing and destructive.

Our hearts are not healthy until they have been satisfied by the only complete, healthy love that exists – that's the love of God Himself. He is the only one who can love unfailingly. There is no love of the natural heart that is safe unless God has first satisfied the human heart.

I was on this journey but I'd never been satisfied by God's love because I couldn't receive it. So why did I think any man could love me correctly? I didn't love myself so how could they love me? You will never have a healthy relationship until you are satisfied by God's love first. That's a powerful message and it took me all these years to learn it.

We are not free to love in the true sense of the word until we have found Love. All of us have looked for love but the important question is where did you search? Who was leading you or who was driving you in the search for unfailing love? If we are lonely and we allow satan to become our tour guide, he will lead us into captivity. I know that from experience. Satan will lead you and guide you into darkness.

We are not wrong to think we need to be loved because we do. But we are wrong to think we can make anyone love us the way we need to be loved. The word of God in I Corinthians 13:8 says, "…God's love is the only love that never fails." It refers to the agape love of God given to us and exercised through us. We all have unmet needs. We carry them around all day long like empty cups. In one way or another, we hold out that empty cup to people in our lives and say, can somebody please fill this? Even a little would help. We'll take a little rejection here. We'll take a little disappointment there. We always want somebody to fill our unmet needs but we never really go to the source. Sometimes we go looking for approval, affirmation, control, success, or gratification but we are still miserable until someone fills our need.

The Bible says, "Let the morning bring me word of Your unfailing love for I have put my trust in you" (Psalm 143:8). I love this scripture so much and I appreciate it because it has brought so much healing to me. It was not until I let the Lord fill my cup of unmet needs with His love that I was satisfied. I had to learn how to receive His love and how to put my trust in Him. I didn't know how to do those things but I learned through the things I suffered. I learned so much about His love that today I can show His love to others. God showed me the way to go, for my life was so miserable and my soul was so wounded. My soul needed to be re-anchored in Him. A heavy yoke was shattered when I brought my heart, mind, soul and all my needs to the Father because I offered Him that empty cup and He filled it with Himself. I didn't ask Him to fill it with things but I asked Him to fill it with Himself and His presence.

No one is more pleasurable to be around than someone whose cup has been filled with the presence of God.

Chapter 12

Overcoming Deception

Let's talk a little bit about deception. When a person has been rejected from the root, there are a lot of materials to tear down from that house the enemy has built. Deception is the glue that holds every stronghold together. However, there is nothing more powerful than God. Therefore anything, other than God, mastering the Christian's life can keep its grip only through the deception of satan who is the father of all lies. There is no truth in him (John 8:44). He specializes in twisting and lying until it seems true.

The list of lies we often believe while being held in our stronghold can be unlimited. I could never be victorious over compulsiveness. I remember the judge told me that I was a very compulsive person and I lived those words out. I've been this way too long and can't change or help myself. It was my stronghold but it was also my pet demon because I needed it to get by. I was worthless. I was nothing but a failure. I thought I was in control, yet it was controlling me. Boy, how many times did I say that? It's not controlling me because I'm in control. This was nothing but deception. I thought I knew just when to stop because I thought I had this thing pegged. There was nothing wrong with my relationship; it was just the church. No one understood me. People just thought evil things about me most of the time. I'm only human. I'm too dysfunctional to even think about being healed. It was my emotions stirring. God couldn't possibly fill the void in my life because I needed something more.

Sometimes we're very aware of tolerating lies but, most of the time, we flow with the deception in our lives. We're caught in such a web that we can no longer see our situation or ourselves accurately. It's not always clear when we're being deceived. One sure sign is when we begin to deceive ourselves. All we have to do is locate the father of lies, satan, by asking the Holy Spirit to show us the lie. Anything we believed that is contrary to the truth of God's word is a lie. We find that in 2 Corinthians 4:2 He tells us how to respond. We have to renounce secret and shameful ways. We should not distort God's word.

This part of my life showed me how to identify satan's lies that needed to be renounced. I renounced all rejection, in order to walk in victory. I renounced shame, deception and distortion of scripture. Our Father of mercy wanted to loose me from the door of secrecy and bring me into a healthy place of joy, peace and freedom but satan wanted to keep me bound in secrecy where he could weigh me down with guilt, misery and shame. I know from experience that much of my shame was wrapped up in pride. The enemy knew that once the secret of the lie was exposed to the light of God's word, I was on my way to freedom.

As you know, my father rejected me. He left me abandoned and I never got to see him. He left the door open for a rejected life. I want to tell you about one of the people in the Bible who knew about a father's rejection. His father, brother, King Saul, his wife, close friends and his son, Absalom, all rejected David. Jesse did not have David at the meeting with Samuel along with his other sons. But God looks on the heart of man when making His decision to anoint someone. It's so funny how a father looked at his own son as just a shepherd boy. He didn't look at him as great. He looked at the other ones as great, but he looked at David as being short, scruffy and not worthy to be anointed as the king. Even when it appears you have been rejected or left out by your parents, God has not left you out. "When my father and my mother forsake me, then the Lord will take me up." (Psalm 27:10) God will never leave you out.

Rejected people look for acceptance from the wrong people. They will not recognize the generosity of their true friends nor will they appreciate those who really love them. I have seen them reject their godly friends only to be controlled and dominated by self-serving manipulators such as Jezebel, Ahab and Balaam. In I Samuel 8:19, Samuel felt the people were rejecting him but God showed Samuel that they weren't really rejecting him; they were rejecting God.

When we are hit with feelings of rejection, it is important not to internalize those feelings. We have to stop taking other people's stuff and making it our own. Rejection builds internal walls to keep love from getting through. Rejected people feel unworthy and they think others view them as unworthy too. When we pray and declare that we are worthy, we tear down the house of rejection that satan built. There is power in our mouths when we learn to receive what God the Father God has done for us.

Sadie Brunson

Chapter 13
Marriage #4

My fourth marriage was another part of my journey. I was the happiest woman in the world because I'd finally met someone who seemed so much like me. I was able to be real with him as I talked about pain. He was a person who had been rejected as well. Uh oh, I attracted another person who was rejected just like me. Wow, I should have known it was going to be such warfare!

I waited seven years before I got married again. I was so happy about it because I'd never waited on God before. I had dealt with a few things but not everything, of course. I could only deal with what God gave me. When I finished Bible school, Pastor Gary spoke a word over me when I walked across the stage. He said, "God will make room for your gift." I received that and God has made a lot of room for me in His kingdom.

At first, the marriage seemed great. We were able to go to the prisons and do street ministry together. This is what we did while we dated; we did all the things of the kingdom. It was so exciting because we would go and speak to the young people together. We were just so busy being little ministers. Pastor Gary counseled us for ten weeks. Also, Myles Munroe taught a marriage class at my beauty shop.

We dealt with a lot of things before marriage. We knew we both had baggage but we had a great relationship because we could communicate. Yes, I saw a few signs that I was more mature than he was but that didn't bother me because he seemed very teachable. He seemed like a person who loved to change.

I prayed a lot about marrying him and the word I got from the Lord was, "I'll take you through it." But He didn't tell me not to marry him. So I prayed right up until the last day. At that time, I had some really great friends like Forest, Danise, B.T., Mary, Faye and Jean. These people were in my life at that time and they were all a part of the wedding party. It was an awesome thing for them to come together because they prayed for me. It was so wonderful!

Pastor Faye was like my mother. She did so much for me. She had the church so beautifully decorated that I couldn't believe all of this was for me. She bought new carpet and wallpaper as if it was her own daughter getting married. It was such an exciting time for me.

I asked Mary to do the circle of love. That's where both families get together and pray to break generational curses and declare that we walk together as one. We went through all of that and it was the most beautiful wedding ever. There were 500-600 people in attendance to witness this wedding and reception. We went to Mexico on our honeymoon and I just knew I was going to have the time of my life. But when I woke up that morning and got close to him he said, "Can't you stay on your side of the bed?" I thought he was playing at first but he was dead serious. Oh no, not another rejection. He rejected me on our honeymoon! I was devastated. I thought I was losing my mind. I thought to myself, "Oh, my God, I couldn't have blown it this time!" I began to pray. I'd had great people speak into my life to make sure I was in the will of God. The Bible says in Proverbs 15:22, "without counsel purposes are disappointed: but in the multitude of counselors they are established." I did all that and what happened? I was rejected...again.

Mercy Rewrote My Life

It was the worst week of my life. I wanted to get out of Mexico but I couldn't. I had to stay there. But I want you to know that the Lord was so gracious. He gave me the grace to deal with it. We came home but I felt like I didn't know the person I'd married. On the wedding tape, he promised that he would never hurt me but that's all he did was hurt me. Before we got married, he'd been offered a job in Texas. He told both the pastors and me that he wasn't going to go but he left immediately. I was left alone, with more rejection.

I had to deal with a lot at this point. I prayed and cried for a whole year. I went through some rough times. I had so much pride that I was ashamed to tell anybody how he treated me. He wouldn't pay the mortgage for about three months or do anything else. He told me that the wedding cost him so much money he didn't have any money left to pay the mortgage. He told me it was my fault and I needed to pay the mortgage myself. I had to endure all of that. It felt like I was in a bad dream. I wanted to wake up from it but it was real. I took as much as I could take but I didn't know what to do. I saw Laurie and told her that I needed to talk to Pastors Gary and Faye. They must have felt that it was urgent because it was New Year's Eve and they told us to bring our clothes to church to get dressed for the gala that night. Pastors Faye and Gary talked to us but I didn't really tell them the truth. I can't remember what I told them but I said something and they agreed to see us.

When they met with us, they gave great counsel. They never took sides. They asked my husband, "Did God change His mind about anything?" You know how people say one thing and then do another. It was always God said this but then they acted like God changed His mind. They brought us both to repentance and we had a good evening after that. Pastor Gary brought forth an awesome word and we partied and ate all night long. We had such a wonderful time on that New Year's Eve.

That night, we left to go to Pittsburgh and had a nice time for about three days. Then his demon came back. He was very distant and cold to me as we were driving home. I soon realized it was because he wasn't delivered from his issues. The change only lasted for a few days and then he went right back to his old flesh.

That was part of my journey. One thing I can truly say is that I didn't let it stop me. I kept on going because God kept opening doors for me to minister. I was so busy. During this process, I learned how to leave people where they were, which I did very well. During that time in my life, the Lord was really showing me things that I didn't want to see. He showed me that He had taken care of me for seven years but I always wanted to be married. I loved being married even though I didn't have such great marriages. I still had some good times. I was a person who loved to serve and enjoyed being a wife. It was a desire I had. I never had a real father and I always looked up to male images. I only had the imaginary father I made up and lied about to the kids. I always said he was working or traveling somewhere. Maybe that's what I was called to be, a wife. Who knows? But I do know, it was the beginning of God showing me how to love the unlovable.

He treated me so badly. I'd never been so rejected by a man. We had wonderful times together as man and wife coming together but then he would reject me as if I was nothing. He would make me feel like I was nothing. He would just move out of the room for no reason – no argument, no nothing – because of his own issues. He would take me on all these trips, because he traveled a lot, but he would treat me badly. He just kept rejecting me.

I was in New Orleans on another miserable trip with my husband and I just left him there. I went to the beauty shop, got a massage and had a good day without him. The next thing I knew he had called all the beauty shops and found out where I was. He apologized for how awful he'd acted. I would never let it cripple me because there was a strength God had given me to go on.

One day, the Lord told me to learn how a prostitute and a whore were treated. So I called my friend, Danise, and asked her to look for some information on the subject for me. I found out that my husband's former lifestyle as a pimp caused him to treat me that way as a method of control. They deny women and then want the women to beg them. That's what pimps do. Well, I learned the game real quick. As much as I cared for him and wanted to be with him, I learned I still wanted somebody who wanted me. It was a very hard thing for me because none of my husbands had ever rejected me sexually. It was very hard to be married to someone and not be able to be intimate, especially since you enjoyed each other. It was the most demonic thing that could've ever happened to me as a woman. Emotionally, it was very damaging to me.

After I finished crying for about a year, I learned more about him. He was wounded too. I learned he had issues with females and that I reminded him of his grandmother who was very stern. He was jealous of me because I had wonderful children and my kids were very respectful in a lot of areas. They were grown then and had their own opinions. That was really a challenge for me because they didn't always agree with me. It made it look like I was the one who was wrong in the house. I felt like I was the controller or the bad person. It turned out, it wasn't like that at all. My youngest daughter lived with me then. One day, she saw me in the hall and said, "Mom, be quiet. I see how he treats you. He treats me and Jazz very well but he has an issue with you. When he lashes out at you, don't say anything back to him." That was like God was saying to me, "Don't say anything, I will expose him."

It was awesome how the Lord allowed me to love him in spite of the way he treated me. It's easy to love someone who loves you, but it's hard to love someone who rejects you and makes you feel like you're less than a woman. Someone who doesn't even make you feel pretty. And, at that time, I think I looked rather nice. I didn't realize that it was an assignment from the pit of hell to make me fall. But this time, I was stronger than I'd ever been. I didn't waver under the pressure because I kept my eyes on Jesus. I don't know what it was but there was something about that time. I didn't even think about stealing. I just went on with my life. I went on with the ministry and the ministry grew. But, in spite of his behavior, I still loved that man and tried to help him day after day. Throughout the rest of our marriage, I tried to show him that there was a better way to live.

Sometimes we talked and he told me I was a great wife and that he loved me. He said I taught him everything he knew and he thanked me. But I guess it wasn't the right time. He's grown a lot now but going through it back then was extremely difficult. When I served Lester Sumrall's wife, she taught on having a meek and quiet spirit. I went to her and said, "I want a meek and quiet spirit." She said, "You have it but you have to mature in that area." I tried really hard to mature in that area by not saying everything that I wanted to say; but sometimes I still found myself saying hurtful things that I was sorry about later. Eventually, I learned not to say everything because the Lord would let me see so much pain in him. He was a needy person who wanted love but didn't know how to receive love. He told me that when we were in marriage counseling, it hurt him when I told Pastor Gary that I didn't love him but I respected him. I really didn't love him. I think it takes a while to love somebody.

I always thought about how it was with Jesus. I didn't love Him either but He loved me. I had to learn how to love Him. Unfortunately, I looked at my husband the same way. I had to learn to love him because we hadn't gone through anything at that time. When we went through, then I could say I truly loved him because God gave me the grace to deal with him. Moreover, God gave me the grace to look beyond his faults because I didn't want to divorce him. I just knew God would heal our marriage and heal us.

He would withhold money from me but he would pay the bills. However, sometimes the Lord would make him give me money. He stood up in church and said, "When I bless my wife, I get blessed." He told me I taught him how to give. I had a lot of good qualities and so did he; however, he hadn't been tested on those qualities yet. He was a very intelligent man and a quick learner. He had a lot of head knowledge but he hadn't actually lived through the things he taught. We were a great team because he was an administrator and I was a worker. I saw so many great things that we could have done as husband and wife for God. I respected him in the kingdom of God. That's really what I loved about him. I had friends who laughed at him because he wore loud clothes but that was his style. I could look beyond all the things he did because there was a beautiful man inside of him wrapped in rejection and abandonment. It broke my heart because I was immature. I married him because I saw someone who I thought loved me and was willing to live his life with me. It was wonderful dating him because we did so much for the kingdom of God together.

I don't believe those things were lost because I believe God was still working on me as I learned to love him. It made a better person out of me. I thank God because the rejection I experienced took me to another part of my life and caused me to deal with it. That's when the Lord told me I had the root of rejection which was so large, like an oak tree. It took a lot of prayers and a lot of years to tear down that root, but I thank the Father for giving me His grace and His mercy. I look back over that today and say, "Father, thank you!"

When I got my divorce, I was on a mission trip in New York. I didn't really deal with the divorce but, believe me, I was deeply hurt.

It was a terrible feeling when he divorced me. It had a big effect on my pride. He really didn't have any reason to divorce me. That was the year of jubilee and everybody was getting their jubilee except me. I said to God, "Couldn't you heal my marriage?" For once, I knew I obeyed God. When my husband was diagnosed with cancer of the mouth, the Lord told him that, if he treated me right, He would heal him. It's all on tape during a service he was preaching in Texas. He started treating me really well and God blessed him. Our whole church at Victory rallied around us and they had a special service for him. His family came all the way from Pittsburgh the day he had surgery. Pastors Gary and Faye and their family came to pick us up and they stayed with us at the hospital the whole time. Pastor Faye never left our sides. I had never seen anything like the kind of love she showed towards us. She was much more excited than me when the doctor came out and said that he didn't have to remove his face. He said the Lord told him to cut him through his lips.

Mercy Rewrote My Life

It was a miracle that the operation was a success. All of the cancer was removed. I thought that after the surgery was over, I was going to have a great marriage which would be second to none. But to my surprise, three days after his surgery, he hated me again. He treated me so badly and told me not to come visit him anymore. After the surgery, he moved out of the house and didn't even tell me. His secretary called me from Texas and said, "I'm so sorry that you and your husband are separated." I didn't even know it.

I hadn't done anything to make him leave me but His demon told him all kinds of things about me. But God is still God and He is so faithful. Today, I don't believe he's like that anymore. When he comes around me, he's very nice. Once, after we were divorced, I was on my way to hear Bishop Jakes speak in Philadelphia. He took me to the bank because he wanted to give me some money. He gave me quite a bit of money and told me he was sorry that I was going through and sorry that he'd abandoned me. I started crying. I never even realized that he had abandoned me too. He asked me to forgive him for abandoning me. And yes, I forgave him because God had forgiven me. We had a great time that day and I had enough money to pay my car payment. The Lord provided for me and I thanked Him over and over again.

I just want to say that all the hurt I went through in that marriage made me who I am today. I understand life more than I ever did and I thank God because I'm not living in that rejected body anymore.

Sadie Brunson

Chapter 14
My Healing

I want to share with you the end of this journey that I've been talking about – my healing. I told you I was going to a church in Ocean City with another great pastor where God used me like I had never been used before in a church. They called me their prophet. God would speak to me about so many things. I really felt good about God using me to speak so often because I didn't have time to think about the divorce much, since I was happy doing the things of God. But when I was alone, I would be very sad. It took awhile to get healed from that because it was so devastating to me.

Before the divorce, I had gone to Atlanta to see my godmother. She asked one of her friends to pray for me. This lady told me I was married to a demon and I had to stop having sex with him because it was controlling me by taking me off focus. I'll never forget what she said because she was the third person who had told me that. And boy, was she right on point! She told me that when I finally stopped submitting my body to him, I would be able to get free from him. She told me it was going to be hard but God had given me the grace to stop. After a while, I stopped desiring him and was able to go on with my life.

When you're sleeping with the enemy, a spirit comes upon you. When you're sleeping with anyone who has a lust spirit, you're sleeping with a controlling spirit. It's a show-off spirit, a "see me, see me" spirit. That's what I attracted. Unfortunately, when you're trapped in rejection like I was, the spirit in you continues to beckon itself. I wondered how I attracted it, but it was a part of my life. I just couldn't help it.

I asked the Lord not to bring another man in my life until I was healed. And He hasn't. There was one guy I met who was a liar. I was so harsh and mean to him. I've never really been mean before but I lashed out at him for every little thing he did. He didn't want to be bothered with me anymore because I was so mean. That was a good thing. I'd asked God not to bring another man in my life until He healed me. I didn't want to hurt another man or be responsible for someone else going through because of me. I haven't dated anyone in over seven years. That's not a bad thing because God has been taking good care of me.

I was on my way to Berlin, MD to go to church. I was in the car with Forest, Danise, Talita and some other people along with their kids. The Lord spoke to me and said, "I want you to go to the church around the corner." I said, "Around the corner? Greater Bethel?" I said to myself, "I know that's not God."

He spoke to me another time and said the same thing but in a much stronger tone. He said, "You're going to get your healing there." I said to myself, "I know that's the devil"; but I obeyed and went that Sunday anyway. When I went it was a nice service so I kept going because He told me to go. Before the next year rolled around (2000), the Holy Spirit told me to join the church. I didn't want to join that day because I was tired from preaching earlier. When I went to church, I sat in the back, which is something I never do. I really didn't want to join but the Lord spoke to me and said, "He's going to be your father and you're going to be established here." I didn't understand that but I got up and went to Bishop Weeks. I walked right up the center aisle. It seemed like such a long walk but he embraced me and he was very grateful. I remembered walking down the steps after service. I could feel the spirits in the church. I began to cry. I said, "God why would you make me join this place? The people aren't happy here." I could tell because I'm very sensitive in the spirit realm. I cried so much but I still obeyed God. He promised me my deliverance and healing were going to come.

Well I complained for a year until one day when I was downtown, an evangelist from the church who works in the city building, heard me complaining about being at Greater Bethel. I told her that the people at this church don't have any love and they're so cold. Nor was the worship enjoyable like I would want it to be. I was just really complaining. I was used to awesome worship and people hugging at the door and loving on one another. This lady said to me, "You're here because of the love you have. We need love and that's why God sent you to us." I was able to receive that response and I asked God to give me the grace not to complain anymore.

One Sunday when I'd first joined the church, I sat beside a young woman named Marsha. There was a connection in the spirit realm. I gave her a word and embraced her and we're still embracing today. We started hanging out together and I thank God for Marsha because she has shown herself to be a true friend to me. I never thought she would be the one. Just like I didn't know my spiritual dad would be Bishop Weeks. I didn't know he would be the one to speak life into me. It's funny how God does things when we think we know, but we don't. I thank God for Marsha's understanding and her faithfulness to me. There's nothing I can ask her that she wouldn't do for me. She's very respectful to me and she's always told me that we're going places. She always saw the gift in me and she always respected me. I don't think we've ever had a bad word between us or even a misunderstanding. I thank the Lord because she's still there for me and we can talk about anything. I thank the Lord for her.

Before I say my healing has come, there's a part of my journey that I must share. I found myself in prison again. This time, when I was locked up, the security guard was a Christian. I never thought I would tell this story but the Lord said I want you to write about the life of a thief and how I protected you.

It's so funny how God's ways are not our ways. I'm not making any excuses; I'm just telling you the truth. This is something I'm not proud of but I pray that you get something out of it because God has forgiven me and loved me through all of it. I want to share it with you because I believe it will help you if you're struggling with something or you know someone else who has a problem with stealing. There are a lot of things you can steal – relationships, people's gifts or even from the church. There are multiple ways that you can steal a whole lot of stuff in those areas.

But back to the story. I found myself back in prison. The security guard was very nice but then the state police came and they were very nasty to me. They put handcuffs on me from the back and took me to lockup to question me. They saw I had a bad record and they made me stay the night in prison without bail or anything. I had to see a detective and she was just as nasty as the police had been. She said, "You're going to prison this time and don't even think you're going to get out." But God spoke to me and said, "You will get out tomorrow morning and you're going to preach tomorrow night." I asked, "How can I preach?" He said, "You'll preach tomorrow night, Saturday and Sunday." I said, "God, how can I do that?" He said, "This is what you did but it's not who you are." I got so quiet. I said, "This is not who I am?" He said, "No." He said, "I'm going to set you free." I just started crying. I said, "When, God? I'm so ashamed. I'm just so ashamed." He said, "Call your daughter." I said, "Oh

God, I can't call her." I didn't want to call anybody but if I was going to call someone, it would have been my girlfriend Gladys, in Chester, because I knew she wouldn't judge me and wouldn't tell a soul. I knew she loved me.

There were other people I thought about calling but God told me to call my daughter, Marlene. I called her and she wasn't very happy about it. I didn't blame her. I didn't want to put that burden on Marlene but God told me to call her, so I did. When I called Marlene, it made it worse for me. The enemy just wore me out. God came into this place and kept talking to me and telling me what to do tomorrow but I couldn't receive it because I was so messed up. I said, "God, suppose Bishop Weeks finds this out? Suppose other people find out what I've done?" The Lord said, "You're worried about people but they don't care about you being here. This is something I allowed to happen." He told me again, "This is what you did but it's not who you are."

I had to sleep on a bed with no mattress. It was cold and hard. It was such a miserable night for me but I fell asleep sometime that morning. They woke me up early and, to my surprise, there was a new detective. He said, "I'm going to get you out of here today." I said, "You are?" He said, "Yes." I said, "But, I'm guilty." He said, "That's okay, I'm going to get you out." He said, "We're going to have court right here. We're not going to take you to court." He told me exactly what to say. I went in before the board and said what he told me to say. They let me sign my own bail and took me to get my car. God took me through that difficult time in my life and I am still amazed at how it all worked out.

Just like God told me, I went the next day and preached. I also preached on Saturday and Sunday. It was a long, very expensive legal process, but He had friends help me pay the money. It took over a year to finish paying it but God took care of me. The first day I went to court, I found out I couldn't get a public defender. I had to get a paid lawyer and they were telling me how much the lawyer would cost. I started crying again. A light-skinned man in a police uniform stopped me as I was walking through the gate. He asked me what was wrong and I told him. He said, "I'm going to help you. Come over here." He was working the door like a security guard. He called an attorney and he came immediately. I told him what happened to me. I was so embarrassed because this attorney was also a deacon in my church. But he told me he was going to help me. He told me what his fee was and it didn't seem that bad at first, until he began to read my record. Then his price went up even more.

I went back with a card to thank the security guard but no one knew who he was. He'd told me his name but no one there had ever heard of him. Now, I know it was an angel. I didn't know who I was then but I know who I am today. I've always attracted the spirit of rejection but now I'm noticing that I've changed after going through so much disappointment. God even showed me how somebody tried to discredit my name and tell people about my fall but it only blessed me. God told me not to say a word about it. He said, "I'll take care of it." And He has.

God has healed me today and given me a new start. I'm attracting people who are awesome and who come to me with something to offer. People who don't just take from me. God is bringing people into my life who really love me. I thank God for all the things I've gone through.

One day, Marsha and I were going to a retreat and she said, "You'll never go back with your husband and you'll never be able to work again because God's going to teach you how to trust Him." That was a very harsh word and I didn't want to hear it because I thought I knew how to trust Him already. I still wanted God to heal my marriage but those words she said are still with me today. They were right on it. She knew God had something much better for me. She knew God was going to take care of me and that I didn't have to worry anymore.

I'm glad I obeyed God because my healing has come. I'm pastoring a church now even though I hated it at first. I felt so unworthy and so ashamed, but God let me know, "I called you to be a pastor because you have such a shepherd's heart." He also told me He would get all the garbage out of my life and put people with me who were respectful, faithful and who would help me and not think they were better than me. Now I'm happy to be a pastor and I'm so happy to be able to go to New Destiny Fellowship (formerly Greater Bethel) every Sunday before I go to my church. I still go to New Destiny because God told me to do so. I thank God for my family at New Destiny and I thank the Lord for the things I walked through because now I see that my healing has come.

Every time I hear my spiritual father speak, he speaks life to me. He's doing something no one has ever done for me before and I take every word personally when I'm listening to the man of God speak. He's taught me so much and I appreciate the God in him.

I'll never forget the first time I went to see Bishop Weeks. It was such a Divine connection. One of the things he told me was that God was going to bring me into a very serious season of separation and that I would have to walk alone. He told me that he had Mrs. Weeks to walk with but he told me that God wanted me to walk alone and depend on Him. It was like God just opened my eyes and I was able to see truth for the first time. I was able to see deception and phoniness.

I was able to see like I've never seen before. God showed me I had been delivered from my past.

I looked for deliverance all over the place but I thank and praise God that He sent me to New Destiny Fellowship and I am delivered today.

Chapter 15

God's Mercy

As long as I live, I don't think I'll ever comprehend why God has allowed me the unspeakable joy of serving him through full-time ministry. God knows I didn't deserve it but my entire life has been a mission of His mercy. I am increasingly awed over my salvation, healing and restoration. I am experiencing total wholeness – spirit, soul, and body.

Rise up in your spirit and rule over your feelings and emotions because you don't have to be bound by hurts from your past any longer. God wants to set you free through His Word. He wants to reveal any past hurts or unconfessed sins, cleanse those wounds with His blood, pour in the oil and wind of the Holy Spirit, totally heal you and make you whole.

To receive healing and live in victory over deep hurts in your life, the first step you must take is to RECOGNIZE the feelings and emotions that are trying to take hold in your life. The very moment someone mistreats, hurts or wounds you, choose to be a VICTOR, not a victim. Refuse to react in the flesh and refuse to give satan an opportunity to gain a stronghold in your life. As Paul told the Romans, "but put ye on the Lord Jesus Christ, and make not provision for the flesh, to fulfill the lust thereof." (Rom. 13:14).

Don't make any provision or allowances for your flesh to react in anger, self-pity, bitterness, resentment, unforgiveness or revenge toward those who have hurt you. Put a stop to the flesh by taking control of your feelings and emotions. You may feel like lashing out in anger and unforgiveness, or you may feel like holding a grudge but don't make any provision for the flesh. God does not expect us to deny or ignore our feelings and emotions because it's natural to have them. But we do not have to allow our feelings to control us.

There are many Christians who have experienced deep hurts but they have failed to recognize and deal directly with their feelings. They are afraid that if they acknowledge that they have been hurt or honestly express their true feelings, other Christians will judge them with word, lack of faith or negative confessions; so they hide their deep hurts behind a mask.

Because of various teachings within the Church, there are many who tell you to just get over it and let it go but they don't tell you how. Many believe Christians should always have a smile on their faces, always be spiritually up and never have a problem. If they do have a problem, it must be because their faith is weak. As a result, many Christians have tried to ignore or deny their feelings because of fear of what other Christians will say to them. They are pretending they are not hurting, pretending they are not depressed or discouraged, pretending they are walking in faith and victory when they actually desperately need to be set free from the past and healed of their deep wounds.

On the outside they are smiling but deep down they are full of despair and hopelessness. They are ready to give up and many are so miserable that they are trying to find a way to take their own lives. I'm not talking about the unsaved. I'm talking about men and women who have been born again, faithful members in churches.

It's time to take the masks off and stop pretending as though we have it all together. It's time to deal directly, openly and honestly before God about our feelings and the deep hurts in our lives. God has made full provision for us to experience healing so we can be WHOLE – spirit, soul, and body. God's promise to us today is healing. "For I will restore health unto thee, and I will heal thee of thy wounds, saith the LORD." (Jeremiah 30:17a). Before we can experience healing of our deep hurts, we must be totally honest with ourselves and God, recognize our feelings and deal with them in the Spirit.

Confess your feelings and hurts to God. Pour out your feelings to Him because He is the only one who can heal your wounded spirit. If you are holding on to feelings of anger, resentment or bitterness towards someone who has hurt you in the past – an unfaithful husband or wife, a rebellious child, an abusive parent, an employer, a controlling pastor or another member of the Body of Christ – confess it openly before God.

It may be that you have become bitter or disappointed or even angry towards God because it's been so long and you still have not received an answer to your prayer. Don't try to hide your feelings from God for He knows your innermost feelings and thoughts anyway. Don't give satan an opportunity to keep you in the stronghold of your life by going around complaining and speaking words against God or against those who have hurt you from the bitterness of your spirit. Open your heart and pour out your feelings to Him. Ask Him to forgive you for holding these feelings in your heart and give you power through the Holy Spirit to get rid of them.

Sadie Brunson

Mercy Rewrote My Life

Prayer:

"In the name of Jesus Christ, I choose to put off the old man and everything that has to do with the old creation nature. I am a new creation in Christ Jesus, old things have passed away and all things have become new. In the name of Jesus who is the Christ, I break, sever, and renounce rejection, pride, lust of the flesh, generational sins, lies and addiction. I rebuke every ungodly soul tie that would bind me to sin or hinder me from growing and maturing and becoming everything that God promised me. I cast down and release myself from every relationship that would prevent me from receiving victory. I declare Jesus Christ is my Victor, my Sanctifier and my Satisfier. I declare Jesus Christ is separating me from the world and the world's system and placing me in righteousness and in the kingdom of God.

I declare every evil soul tie to be broken and destroyed with (*name every person, group or organization that is revealed by the Holy Spirit to your mind*) and I break and loose myself from all their influence, cords, ties, threads, tentacles, webs, bands, agreement, oaths, vows and inner vows in Jesus' name. I break all word curses spoken upon me by them or myself. I declare myself to be bound only by the glorious liberty and truth that comes through Jesus Christ in Jesus' name. Amen.

Isa. 53: 3-4

[3] He was despised and rejected by men,
  a man of sorrows, and familiar with suffering.
  Like one from whom men hide their faces
  he was despised, and we esteemed him not.

[4] Surely he took up our infirmities

and carried our sorrows,
yet we considered him stricken by God,
smitten by him, and afflicted.

Jesus is a man of sorrows who is acquainted with grief and He understands because He's been there and has lived in your sorrow.

John 16:33

[33]"I have told you these things, so that in me you may have peace. In this world you will have trouble. But take heart! I have overcome the world."

Sadie Brunson

About the Author

Pastor Sadie Brunson is a prolific, dynamic, and heavily anointed minister. She brings a warm, compassionate and direct approach to caring for those who have been wounded – troubled by their past – or those who are just plain hungry for God and desire to grow closer to the Lord. Sadie is a consecrated woman of God who walks in a divine flow of God's love and grace. She is loved and cherished by all that know her.

Sadie is especially anointed to help people find their purpose and to aid them in walking in God's ordained plan and giftings. Also, God uses Sadie, under an apostolic anointing, to support those who are called to the ministry. She is equipped to train and mentor men and women for God's service and has been of tremendous inspiration and encouragement to many Pastors throughout this nation and abroad.

After more than twenty years of preaching, teaching, holding deliverance services, conducting prison ministry, and traveling in missions work, God has now called Sadie to launch a church ministry. Sadie is Pastor and Founder of Abundant Love Ministries. For many souls, this ministry will be a place similar to an emergency room, where people will be able to come and receive the spiritual treatment and healing they so desperately need. Every person needs some place – a sort of refuge. Abundant Love Ministries is that place. Sadie takes emergency calls for deliverance ministry, prayer, and/or counseling.

Abundant Love Ministries' services are being held at 30 Germay Drive in Wilmington, Delaware every Sunday at 10:00 a.m. in addition to Intecessory Prayer every Monday at 6:00 a.m. and Bible Study every Wednesday at 7:00 p.m. All are welcome and invited to come and be a part of these truly Spirit-filled services.

Regional "Makeover" classes and conferences are also being established and scheduled throughout the U.S. where many others can experience inner healing through God's love.

Every person that comes under Sadie's care receives special love and attention. No souls are turned away because Sadie knows how important we all are to Jesus and the plan of God.

For more information on the ministry or to book speaking engagements, please contact us at:

Abundant Love Ministries
30 Germay Drive
Wilmington, DE 19804
(302) 654-5059
www.abundant-love-ministries.org
Email: ministry@abundant-love-ministries.org

Notes:

Notes:

Notes:

Notes:

Notes:

Notes:

Notes:

Notes:

Notes: